DOCTOR FAUSTUS
1604

THE MALONE SOCIETY
REPRINTS, VOL. 185
2018

PUBLISHED FOR THE MALONE SOCIETY
BY MANCHESTER UNIVERSITY PRESS

Altrincham Street, Manchester M1 7JA, UK
www.manchesteruniversitypress.co.uk

British Library Cataloguing-in-Publication Data
A catalogue record for this book is available from the British Library

Library of Congress Cataloging-in-Publication Data applied for

ISBN 978–1–5261–2692–4

Typeset by New Leaf Design, Scarborough, North Yorkshire

Printed by in the UK by Henry Ling Limited, at the Dorset Press, Dorchester, DT1 1HD

This edition of *Doctor Faustus 1604* was prepared by Chiaki Hanabusa and checked by Eric Rasmussen, with additional bibliographical assistance from G. R. Proudfoot and H. R. Woudhuysen. The editor wishes to express his thanks to Paul Dean for comments on style. Completion of the edition was facilitated by the award of the Malone Society's Colin Baldwin Fellowship for 2016.

  The Society is grateful to the Bodleian Library, Oxford, for permission to reproduce its unique copy of the play (Arch. A e. 125).

June 2018   PAUL DEAN

         © *The Malone Society 2018*

CONTENTS

Introduction ix
   The 1604 Quarto ix
   The Play's Source and Early History xxiii
   The Printer's Manuscript of the Play xxix
   The Bodleian Copy of the 1604 Quarto xxxiv
Appendix: Edmond Malone's Manuscript Notes on Q1
    Faustus xxxix
List of Roles xli
Obscured and Damaged Readings xliii
The Text 1

INTRODUCTION

The 1604 Quarto

Christopher Marlowe's *The Tragical History of Doctor Faustus* (1604; STC 17429) was first entered in the Registers of the Stationers' Company by Thomas Bushell on 7 January 1601:

> 7. Ianuarij [1600/1]
> **Tho. Busshell**   Entred for his copye vnder the handes. of M^r Dc̃or Barlowe, and the Wardens. A booke called the plaie of Dc̃or ffaustus   vj^{d}[1]

The entry shows that, by paying six pence as the licence fee, Bushell, publisher and bookseller, acquired permission to publish the play and that he established the ownership of the title—that is, he gained the exclusive right to publish (and republish) it. The record also implies that he paid four pence directly to the Clerk as the registration fee for writing the entry. This fee was not recorded because it was the Clerk's personal fee and not part of the Wardens' accounts. Bushell could have saved four pence if he had wished to, for entrance was optional, while permission to print was legally mandatory. It is clear from the entry that Bushell paid a total of ten pence to the Company to acquire permission, licence, and entrance.[2]

The licenser was William Barlow (d. 1613), successively Bishop of Rochester (1606–8) and Bishop of Lincoln (1608–13). He matriculated at St John's College, Cambridge, in 1580 and received his BA in early 1584, the same year that Marlowe graduated from Corpus Christi College, Cambridge, with his BA.[3] In 1596 Barlow, then a fellow of Trinity Hall, preached at Paul's Cross, celebrating the Earl of Essex's victory at Cadiz. This probably impressed Archbishop John Whitgift, who made Barlow his chaplain immediately afterwards. With this promotion, Barlow started his career as an ecclesiastical licenser, presumably to help Whitgift reduce his burden of licensing books. Yet Barlow was not simply a licenser but a prolific theologian and preacher. Between 1596 and 1613, he published thirteen titles comprising, among other

---

[1] W. W. Greg, *A Bibliography of the English Printed Drama to the Restoration*, 4 vols (London, 1939–59), 1.17. See also Edward Arber, *A Transcript of the Registers of the Company of Stationers of London, 1554–1640 A.D.*, 5 vols (London and Birmingham, 1875–94), 3.178. *STC* references are to A. W. Pollard and G. R. Redgrave, *A Short-Title Catalogue of Books Printed in England, Scotland, and Ireland and of English Books Printed Abroad, 1475–1640*, 2nd edn, revised and enlarged by W. A. Jackson, F. S. Ferguson, and Katharine F. Pantzer, 3 vols (London, 1976–91).

[2] For details of permission, licence, and entrance, see Peter W. M. Blayney, 'The Publication of Playbooks', in *A New History of Early English Drama*, ed. John D. Cox and David Scott Kastan (New York, 1997), 383–402, pp. 398–405.

[3] For Barlow's biography, see W. W. Greg, *Licensers for the Press, &c. to 1640: A Biographical Index Based Mainly on Arber's 'Transcript of the Registers of the Company of Stationers'*, Oxford Bibliographical Society, NS 10 (Oxford, 1962), pp. 9–10, 81, 109; Greg, *Bibliography*, 3.1480; C. S. Knighton, 'William Barlow (d. 1613)', in *Oxford Dictionary of National Biography Online* (*ODNB*) (http://www.oxforddnb.com/), accessed 4 June 2017. For Marlowe's degree, see Lisa Hopkins, *A Christopher Marlowe Chronology* (Basingstoke, 2005), p. 67.

items, his own sermons at Paul's Cross, a translation of a German sermon, and a report of the Hampton Court Conference.[4]

By 1606 when he was elevated to the see of Rochester, Barlow is recorded to have licensed fifty-five titles in all, of which *Faustus* was the thirtieth in his career.[5] The books he licensed comprise his own sermons and those of others, treatises on theology, and books on history and foreign affairs, notably the first edition of Francis Bacon's *Essays* (1597; STC 1137–7.5) and the first quarto of William Shakespeare's *Richard III* (1597; STC 22314).[6] *Essays* and *Richard III* are two of the very few books he licensed that could be categorized as literature. Barlow would have encountered Marlowe's name when he inspected Thomas Beard's *The Theatre of God's Judgements* (1597; STC 1659). On 27 November 1596, three and half years after Marlowe's death, Barlow issued a licence for the book,[7] in which Beard described, in a section entitled 'Of Epicures and Atheists', how '*Marlin*' of 'fresh and late memory', who 'denied God and his sonne Christ', was stabbed to death as 'a manifest signe of Gods iudgement' (sig. K5^{r-v}). In June 1599, Whitgift and the Bishop of London ordered the Stationers' Company to ban and burn several books, of which Sir John Davies's *Epigrams and Elegies* (*c*.1599; STC 6350–0.5), which included Marlowe's translation of some of Ovid's *Elegies*, was one.[8] This unusual suppression of books by ecclesiastical censorship no doubt obliged Barlow to pay particularly cautious attention to Marlowe. It seems hard, then, to resist the view that Barlow had an image in his mind of Marlowe as an unlawful poet. In 1600, only a year after copies of Marlowe's *Elegies* had been burnt in public, Barlow licensed another book that was slightly linked to the poet. This was *England's Helicon*, a large collection of pastoral and lyrical poetry (1600; STC 3191).[9] Among the scores of poems that it contained, including pieces by Philip Sidney and Shakespeare, was Marlowe's 'The passionate Sheepheard to his loue' (sigs 2A1^v–2^r). Doubtless Barlow was one of the earliest Renaissance readers of *Faustus* in manuscript form, apart from the actors and other theatrical personnel (for the nature of the manuscript, see below). When he received the play's handwritten text, Barlow was Rector of St Dunstan-in-the-East in London (1597–1606). If he thought of Marlowe as a blasphemous and

---

[4] His sermons preached before Queen Elizabeth were reported by Sir John Harington to have been 'manie and verie good', one of which she 'liked exceedingly' remarking that 'his talke may teach you all in Court'. When Barlow was Bishop of Rochester, Harington counted him as 'one of the rypest in learning of all his Predecessors'. See *Sir John Harington: A Supplie or Addicion to the Catalogue of Bishops, to the Yeare 1608*, ed. R. H. Miller (Potomac, Md., 1979), pp. 142–3.

[5] The number of titles licensed by him corrects Greg's count of fifty-three in *Licensers for the Press*, pp. 9, 81. Barlow's titles and family name were variably inscribed in the Registers as 'master/master Doctor', 'Barlow/Barlowe/Barloe/Barlay/Barley', or 'the Bishop of Rochester'. After he had taken a doctorate in theology in 1599, he was usually called 'master Doctor'.

[6] Barlow licensed three of his own sermons (STC 1447, 1451, 1454). This must have been an unusual but efficient system for Barlow and the Stationers' Company. For the entries of *Essays* and *Richard III*, see Arber, *Transcript*, 3.79, 93, respectively.

[7] Arber, *Transcript*, 3.75.

[8] For details of the Bishops' Ban, see Arber, *Transcript*, 3.677–8; Cyndia Susan Clegg, *Press Censorship in Elizabethan England* (Cambridge, 1997), pp. 198–217.

[9] Arber, *Transcript*, 3.168.

corrupting writer, it is highly likely that Barlow perused the original manuscript carefully. The last licence he had given before *Faustus* was to a historical work that was entered on 10 October 1600.[10] It is a reasonable inference that he finished licensing *Faustus* after that date. That is, his decision to give permission for the play that we have now to be printed was eventually made at some point between mid-October 1600 and the first week of January 1601. Barlow 'died somewhat sodainely' as Bishop of Lincoln on 7 September 1613.[11]

It was three years after the entry that the earliest extant edition of *Faustus* was published. This was a quarto edition printed by Valentine Simmes for Bushell. The first quarto (hereafter Q1) has traditionally been labelled the 'A-text' (as against the later revised and expanded 'B-text'). Only a single copy of Q1, formerly owned by Edmond Malone, survives; it is now housed in the Bodleian Library (Arch. A e. 125, formerly Mal. 233 (3)).[12] The play was reprinted in 1609. The publisher of Q2 (STC 17430) switched from Bushell to John Wright, publisher and bookseller, and the printer from Simmes to George Eld. Presumably, before Q2 was issued Bushell and Wright had reached a private agreement of some sort about its publication and ownership. The 'indirect dealing' between the two stationers, as this was often called in the Stationers' Registers, was formally recorded a year later, on 13 September 1610, when Bushell assigned to Wright the exclusive right to reissue the play.[13] Wright's careful business tactics of searching for promisingly saleable items in advance of publication may have caused the delayed assignment. Subsequently, Wright as the *bona fide* assignee had Eld reprint the play and published it as Q3 (STC 17431) in 1611. In 1616, Wright published the first B-text edition, Q4 (STC 17432), with substantial new additions. Until he retired in 1640–1, Wright published a long series of B-text editions, Q5 (1619; STC 17433), Q6 (1620; STC 17434), Q7 (1624; STC 17435), Q8 (1628; STC 17435.5), and Q9 (1631; STC 17436).[14]

Q1 collates 4°: A–F⁴. The title-page is A1ʳ. The title reads 'THE | TRAGICALL | History of D. Faustus. | *As it hath bene Acted by the Right* | *Honorable the Earle of Nottingham his seruants.* | Written by Ch. Marl.'.[15] Under Marlowe's abbreviated name is a printer's device representing 'A boy with wings upon his right arm and with his left hand holding, or fastened to, a weight'. The device, implicitly signifying 'talent kept from rising by the

---

[10] Arber, *Transcript*, 3.174. The book was William Fulbecke's *An Historical Collection of the Continual Factions of the Romans and Italians* (1601; STC 11412).

[11] Francis Godwin, *A Catalogue of the Bishops of England* (1615; STC 11938), sig. X4ᵛ.

[12] For bibliographical details of the first and all subsequent editions of the play, see STC 17429–36; Greg, *Bibliography*, 1.327–31 (no. 205 (a–j)); Martin Wiggins with Catherine Richardson, *British Drama 1533–1642: A Catalogue: Volume II: 1567–1589* (Oxford, 2012), pp. 419–27 (no. 810); 'ESTC. English Short Title Catalogue', British Library Website (http://www.bl.uk/); 'DEEP: Database of Early English Playbooks' (http://deep.sas.upenn.edu/). The shelfmark of the Bodleian's copy of the play was changed in 2003.

[13] Greg, *Bibliography*, 1.26; Arber, *Transcript*, 3.442.

[14] For Q4 and the B-text editions, see the Malone Society edition of *Doctor Faustus 1616*.

[15] Long-s and ligatures are not reproduced here and elsewhere. Black-letter is reproduced in this Introduction in roman, while roman and italic/swash are reproduced in roman and italic, respectively.

burden of poverty', had been passed to Simmes by 1596 before he used it on the title-page of Shakespeare's *Richard II* (1597; STC 22307). Simmes continued to use it until 1606.[16] Under the device is the title-page imprint, reading 'LONDON | Printed by V. S. for Thomas Bushell. 1604.'. The imprint suggests that Bushell, who presumably procured the manuscript himself as a publishing bookseller, invested in the production of Q1, and that Simmes was hired by him as the printer.[17] A1^v is blank, but in the surviving copy it has a brown ink show-through of 'f' written on A1^r and a set-off of what appears to be a brown exclamation mark written on A2^r (TLN 21). On A2^r is the head-title, 'The tragicall Historie | of Doctor Faustus.', followed by one of Simmes's rectangular ornaments.[18] The text of the play begins at TLN 11, with a centred entry direction for 'Chorus' and a large upper-case roman 'N' (7.0 × 7.0 millimetres) set at the beginning of TLN 12–13. The play ends at TLN 1528 on F3^r. The book's final line of text is a Latin motto '*Terminat hora diem, Terminat Author opus.*' (The hour ends the day, the author ends his work), followed by one of Bushell's devices depicting 'Justice striking a bushel of corn', with an oval frame bearing the motto 'SVCH AS I MAKE SVCH WILL I TAKE'.[19] F3^v is blank, with show-through of the text and Bushell's device. The unique copy lacks the final leaf F4. Q2 was a page-by-page reprint of Q1, except for the design of the title-page and a different printer's ornament on F3^r. Q3 was also a reprint of its predecessors, but the title-page is printed on A2^r and the text runs to F4^r, while the ornament was replaced by 'FINIS.'.

The play was not divided into acts or scenes. The least intrusive editorial policy would divide the text as follows: Chorus 1, Scenes 1–5, Chorus 2, Scene 6, Chorus 3, Scenes 7–9, Chorus 4, Scenes 10–11, and Chorus 5.[20] Although Scene 7 (Robin's book-stealing episode) and Chorus 3 have been considered misplaced, the A-text, as it stands, represents what Jacobean readers actually read. In modern critical editions, the act and scene divisions vary slightly, according to the editor's judgement.[21] In Scene 9, the location changes in succession from the German Emperor's palace to some place near Wittenberg and

---

[16] For the device, see Ronald B. McKerrow, *Printers' & Publishers' Devices in England & Scotland 1485–1640* (London, 1913; reprinted 1949), pp. 51–2 (no. 142). For its use by Simmes, see W. Craig Ferguson, *Valentine Simmes: Printer to Drayton, Shakespeare, [...] and Other Elizabethans* (Charlottesville, VA, 1968), pp. 43, 49.

[17] For interpretation of the imprint, see M. A. Shaaber, 'The Meaning of the Imprint in Early Printed Books', *The Library*, 4th ser., 24 (1943–4), 120–41.

[18] See 'Ferguson 11' (above), in his *Valentine Simmes*, p. 47.

[19] See McKerrow, *Devices*, p. 123 (no. 313); Ferguson, *Valentine Simmes*, p. 44. This device had also appeared in three other books that Simmes printed for Bushell in 1600–2; STC 11578 (1600, on the title-page), STC 20053 (1601, on the title-page and sig. C6^r), and STC 20151 (1602, on the title-page and V8^r).

[20] The scenes occur as follows: Chorus 1 (TLN 11–39), Scene 1 (40–210), Scene 2 (211–52), Scene 3 (253–369), Scene 4 (370–446), Scene 5 (447–818), Chorus 2 (819–30), Scene 6 (831–939), Chorus 3 (940–57), Scene 7 (958–94), Scene 8 (995–1047), Scene 9 (1048–275), Chorus 4 (1276–84), Scene 10 (1285–396), Scene 11 (1397–518), and Chorus 5 (1519–27).

[21] For a useful diagram showing the correspondence of scenes between the A- and B-texts, see, for example, *'The Tragical History of Doctor Faustus': A Critical Edition of the 1604 Version*, ed. Michael Keefer (Peterborough, Ontario, 2008), pp. 128–9.

to the Duke of Vanholt's residence. The carrying over of characters to a different locale within a scene, a 'dramatic *enjambement*', as W. W. Greg termed it, would possibly have been performed using both the inner and outer space of the stage separately to represent various locations.[22]

Each page of sheets A–D has thirty-seven text-lines, including blank lines between speech and stage directions. The depth of the text area, excluding the headline and the direction line, measures 151–4 millimetres. A rare arrangement of blank lines by the compositor (Compositor X, for whom, see below) can be observed in TLN 142–4 (sig. A3^v), where five type-lines can be counted, that is, two lines of speech plus a single-line stage direction with blank lines above and below it. The depth of 13 millimetres measured between the base of lines of TLN 142 and 144 corresponds, in fact, to only four type-lines elsewhere. This probably suggests that Compositor X used two thinner leads above and below the stage direction in order to avoid the somewhat awkward arrangement of leaving a blank line at the foot of the page. In sheets E–F, the compositors (X and Compositor Y) decreased the number of text-lines on each page to thirty-six, with the depth of the page shrinking to 148–51 millimetres, accordingly. E4^r exceptionally has thirty-seven lines. Presumably, before they started setting up sheet E, the compositors re-estimated the length of printed pages necessary to accommodate the remaining text.[23] In other words, to avoid clumsy workmanship, the compositors attempted to recalculate where the final printed page would end. The last thing that they would want was either that the text would overflow sheet F, or that composition would finish at the beginning of sheet F, for instance, on F1^r or F1^v.[24] In the former case, Simmes would have had to renegotiate with Bushell about a further supply of paper; in the latter, six or seven out of eight pages would become uselessly blank, causing a waste in production costs. Half-sheet imposition of sheet F might have been another option, but this would also have required renegotiation about the amount of paper.[25] As soon as they finished the composition of sheet D, the compositors probably recalculated roughly how much of the text remained to be set, despite the difficulty of casting-off a large number of prose lines in sheet E (discussed below), and found that, if they kept setting thirty-seven lines per page in sheets E–F, only three or so lines of speech and the Latin motto would be left for the final printed page, F3^r. Such a large white space may have been judged visually intolerable, although some of the gap could have been filled with the three stage directions and Bushell's device. Based on this estimation, the compositors started to set thirty-six lines per page from E1^r in order to increase the printed area on

---

[22] *Marlowe's 'Doctor Faustus' 1604~1616: Parallel Texts*, ed. W. W. Greg (Oxford, 1950), p. 21. See also Walter Wilson Greg, 'Webster's *White Devil*: An Essay in Formal Criticism', *Modern Language Quarterly*, 3 (1900), 112–26, p. 121.

[23] It is certain that the compositors had cast-off the text very roughly for Bushell and Simmes to estimate the amount of paper needed to print Q1. They would have cast-off the copy more precisely shortly before composition.

[24] Philip Gaskell, *A New Introduction to Bibliography* (Oxford, 1972), p. 41, states that casting-off enabled the compositor to make decisions about typographical details so that 'the text would not overrun the last whole sheet by a page or two'.

[25] For half-sheet imposition, see Gaskell, *New Introduction*, p. 83.

F3ʳ by eleven lines (allowing for the extra line of E4ʳ). Although the three blank pages from F3ᵛ to F4ᵛ may appear redundant, by leaving F4 blank, it could be turned back when all sheets were gathered and folded to cover the title-page as a wrapper.[26]

The width of the compositor's measure in sheets A–E is 89–90 millimetres, while in sheet F it is 90.5–91 millimetres. Paper shrinkage probably caused the difference in the width of the measure between sheets A–E and F, since it is likely that a different stock of paper was used to print F (see below). The text is mainly set in pica black-letter fount, called 'textura', with twenty lines measuring 82–3 millimetres. In the first quarter of the sixteenth century, English printers adopted the northern French textura directly from France or Flanders, and the fount gradually became established in England as the ordinary standard type.[27] The black-letter Simmes used to print Q1 was one of the most popular sizes of type-face in Elizabeth's age: it is an eighty-two textura (that is, a textura measuring 82 millimetres in twenty lines).[28] Simmes's black-letter fount contains square upper-case 'T's, although it was mixed with a small number of round 'T's (TLN 28, 186, 548, 737, etc.); they were presumably the remnants of another black-letter fount with a different type-design that he had used temporarily from 1594 to 1597.[29] The black-letter used for Q1 is also remarkable for its added ligatures: the 'ée' ligature has an accent on the first 'e' and was used, for instance, in 'déedes' (TLN 16), 'yéeres' (24), and 'hée' (26), while the 'oo' ligature can be seen in such spellings as 'good' (19), 'soone' (26), and 'mooue' (96). Simmes used this mixed black-letter from 1594 to 1607 for printing a wide range of books, including sermons, news pamphlets, prose romances, and plays such as Q1 *A Warning for Fair Women* (1599; STC 25089) and Thomas Dekker's Q1 *The Shoemakers' Holiday* (1600; STC 6523).[30] Comparison of the number of *STC* items printed by Simmes in black-letter and those printed in roman type makes it clear that the frequency of his use of black-letter shrank over the years. During the first five years of his career (1594–8), more or less half of Simmes's output of about seventy books had the main part of the text set in black-letter and half in roman.[31] During the following five years (1599–1603), black-letter

---

[26] The blank leaf A1 of Q3 was likewise intended to protect the title-page.

[27] H. D. L. Vervliet, *Sixteenth-Century Printing Types of the Low Countries* (Amsterdam, 1968), p. 42; A. F. Johnson, *Type Designs: Their History and Development*, 3rd edn (London, 1966), p. 10.

[28] Frank Isaac, *English Printers' Types of the Sixteenth Century* (Oxford, 1936), pp. 36–7. The design of Simmes's black-letter looks similar to the eighty-three textura used by John Cawood (1513/14–1572), the Queen's Royal Printer: see Isaac, *English Printers' Types*, plate 54.

[29] Ferguson, *Valentine Simmes*, p. 41. Ferguson classified the main fount used to print Q1 as 'B.L.1b' and the mixed-in fount as 'B.L.1a', which was probably discarded in or after 1597.

[30] Of twenty-five plays printed by Simmes, these two and Q1 *Faustus* were the only plays that he printed in black-letter. Ferguson lists the majority of books printed by Simmes with reference to a variety of type-faces and type sizes (*Valentine Simmes*, pp. 42–3).

[31] The number of *STC* items per year is based on *STC*, 3.155, with their main fount checked against Ferguson, *Valentine Simmes*, pp. 42–3 and 'EEBO: Early English Books Online' (https://eebo.chadwyck.com/home), accessed 15 April 2018. Unfortunately, the latter does not reproduce a few *STC* items printed by Simmes, with the result that the counts here are provisional. Nonetheless, it does not seriously affect the following discussion and conclusion.

was used, by contrast, in some seventeen items only, as against approximately sixty-five set in roman. This typographical practice continued during the final seven years of his career (1604–7, 1610–12), when about fifteen were printed mainly in black-letter, while at least fifty-one were printed mainly in roman. The gradual shift in his selection of type-face from black-letter to roman type accords with Frank Isaac's remark that during Elizabeth's reign 'romans and italics reached a stage of perfection which would have been impossible in the preceding reigns'.[32] Of nineteen *STC* items Simmes produced in 1604, Q1 was the only one printed in black-letter. Peter W. M. Blayney states that 'jest-books, works for the instruction and improvement of the young, certain kinds of sensational news pamphlets, and above all, ballads' were usually printed in black-letter.[33] Bushell would probably have deemed *Faustus* a sensational play and so commissioned Simmes to print it in black-letter.

In Q1, roman type in various sizes was also used to print, for instance, the title, the title-page imprint, the head-title, the running-titles, and the opening stage direction 'Enter Chorus.' (TLN 11). Pica roman fount, measuring 82–3 millimetres in twenty lines, was used for printing, in particular, speech-prefixes, proper names, including those of some allegorical characters and those originating from the Bible and classical myths, and others including 'Theologie' (TLN 30), 'Astrologie' (673), 'Saturne', 'Mars', 'Iupiter' (681), and 'Cosmography' (826).[34] Also printed in pica roman were 'all promises' (548) made between Faustus and Mephistopheles (551–66) and the dirge that the friars sing (927–9, 931, 933, 935). This pica roman face was classified as 'Simmes-S1' by Adrian Weiss. Simmes is known to have made use of this type-face for books that he printed between 1594 and 1606, including Shakespeare's Q1 *Richard III* (sheets A–G only).[35] Pica italic type was used for printing part of the name of the dramatic company that performed the play (TLN 5), as well as for stage directions and Latin and other languages in the main text.[36] Elsewhere italic upper-case '*F*' and '*M*' were often used to make up for temporary shortages of their roman equivalents caused by their frequent use in setting the names of Faustus and Mephistopheles. These include, for instance, '*F*austus' (TLN 258, 267, 286, 292, 310, 312, 320, etc.), '*F*au.' (291, 298, 300, 310, 319, 321,

---

[32] Isaac, *English Printers' Types*, p. 35. Johnson, *Type Designs*, p. 10, observes that black-letter's final disappearance as an ordinary body type may be dated to the period of the Civil War.

[33] Blayney, 'The Publication of Playbooks', p. 414.

[34] But black-letter was also used for 'Faustus' (TLN 448, etc.), 'Belsabub' (452, etc.), 'Mephastophilis' (537, etc.), 'Mercury' (693), 'Pride' (751), 'sloath' (795), 'leachery' (804), 'Lucifer' (814), 'France' (837), 'Rome' (885), and 'Florence' (900–1), while '*Sandelo*' (931), '*Faustus*' (1137), '*Greece*' (1288, 1291), '*Troy*', and '*Wertenberge*' (1375) were set in italic.

[35] Adrian Weiss, 'Bibliographical Methods for Identifying Unknown Printers in Elizabethan/Jacobean Books', *Studies in Bibliography*, 44 (1991), 183–288, p. 206. W. Craig Ferguson had classified it as 'Lyon (b) [1a]', in his *Pica Roman Type in Elizabethan England* (Aldershot, 1989), pp. 30–1 and plate 134 (formerly 'ROMAN 1' in his *Valentine Simmes*, pp. 40–2). Ferguson's type-face identification was severely criticised by Weiss in his review of the book in *Papers of the Bibliographical Society of America*, 83 (1989), 539–46, although Weiss agreed with Ferguson that Simmes used it between 1594 and 1606.

[36] Exceptions probably caused by the compositors' inadvertent error include '*exeunt* with him' (TLN 1518) set in both italic and roman.

324, 328, etc.), 'First' (551), 'Fourthly' (556), '*Me.*' (521, 533, 538, 541, etc.), and '*M*ephastophilis' (552, 554, etc.). Isaac states that Simmes's pica italic has 'such a strong resemblance' to that of Christopher Barker (1528/9–99) 'that they seem to have been cast by the same founder'.[37] With this fount, Simmes italicized not only 'The Prologue' (sig. A2ʳ) of Q1 *The First Part of Sir John Oldcastle* (1600; STC 18795), but 'To the Reader' (A2ʳ) and 'An imperfect Ode [...] spoken by the Prologue' (I4ʳ) in John Marston's Q3 *The Malcontent* (1604; STC 17481). Among the 'swash' italic types in the main text are: '*A*' (TLN 69), '*B*' (567), '*C*' (370), '*G*' and '*R*' (995), '*M*' (723), '*P*' and '*T*' (909), '*Q*' (288), and '*V*' (999).

The first three leaves of each sheet of Q1 were signed with black-letter capitals and, on the second and third leaves, with Arabic numerals. Only the title-page and the final page, sig. F3ʳ, were unsigned. The setting of the catchwords is accurate, where it is sufficiently visible. On C3ʳ and E4ʳ, only traces of the tops of the upper-case letters are visible, to such an extent that the catchwords' correctness is indeterminable.[38] The catchword on D3ʳ is invisible, as the direction line was severely trimmed. The only instance where the catchword and the initial word on the following page do not match each other is on A3ʳ⁻ᵛ. The catchword reads 'Than' on A3ʳ, but the word that immediately follows on A3ᵛ is 'Thn' (TLN 110). There are some typographical variations between the catchword and the initial word of the following page that result from the compositors' abbreviation and omission of speech-prefixes and from his use of a different fount and different punctuation marks.[39] The compositors used lower-case 'w' when either upper-case 'W' or its equivalent 'VV' was required for setting the catchword, as can be seen between 'what' (catchword on B4ᵛ) and 'What' (the initial word on B4ᵛ; TLN 475); 'whose' (catchword on D1ʳ) and 'VVhose' (the initial word on D1ᵛ; 841); 'which' (catchword on D2ᵛ) and 'VVhich' (the initial word on D3ʳ; 950), and 'where' (catchword on F2ʳ) and 'Where' (the initial word on F2ᵛ; 1477). The fact that on all four occasions the compositors substituted lower-case 'w' indicates that they were well aware of the need to save 'W's and 'V's in preparation for their frequent use elsewhere. Lower-case type was also used for setting the initial letters of speech-prefixes: for instance, 'emp' (1112, 1116, 1120, 1122, 1133, 1142) for the Emperor, and 'euill' (652, 656, 717, 719) and 'good' (718, 720) for the two Angels to save their upper-case equivalents.

---

[37] Isaac, *English Printers' Types*, p. 42. This is Ferguson's 'ITALIC 1' in his *Valentine Simmes*, p. 42. Barker was Queen's printer of Latin, Greek, and Hebrew, and was one of the most important Elizabethan printers.

[38] Nothing but the upper-right and the upper-left serifs of 'M' can clearly be seen on sig. C3ʳ, while on E4ʳ only the horizontal bar of 'T' is visible.

[39] Abbreviations of speech-prefixes are 'Wagner' (sig. B3ʳ CW) / 'Wag.' (the initial word on B3ᵛ; TLN 403); 'Faustus' (E1ʳ CW) / 'Fau:' (E1ᵛ; 1130); while in 'euill' (C2ᵛ CW) / 'euill An:' (C3ʳ; 656) part of the speech-prefix has been omitted. The use of a different fount can be seen in '*Fau.*' (C1ᵛ CW) / '*Fau.*' (C2ʳ; 583); '*Mu-* [swash italic *M*]' (E3ᵛ CW) / '*Musicke*' (E4ʳ; 1300), and different punctuation marks are used in '*Me:*' (C1ʳ CW) / '*Me.*' (C1ᵛ; 547) and '*Me:*' (D1ᵛ CW) / '*Me.*' (D2ʳ; 878).

The compositors took pains to save space and to prevent the text from overflowing the line. Where they unavoidably had to turn over a speech, they employed turn-downs (TLN 1324–5 and 1503–4). The text was turned up only once, at 857–8, although there was sufficient space to turn it down in the line that immediately follows. The stage directions were usually centred and provided with blank lines above and/or below them (11, 111, etc.) or set without them (40, 104, etc.). However, a large number of directions other than '*exit*' and '*exeunt*' were set in the blank space left after the preceding speech.[40] There are also three short directions composed in two consecutive lines in the right-hand side of the body of the text (1253–4, 1307–8, 1327–8), of which the first two signal entrances. One stage direction, '*exit Meph.*' (1252), is set within a speech spoken by Faustus, as if to emphasize that the action has to begin while Faustus is still speaking. The use of blank space, the right-hand side of the body of the text, and even within a speech for setting directions reveals that, apart from the influence of the copy from which the play was set, the compositors were careful enough, where possible, not to let the directions take up too much space.

Textual flaws abound, such as misspellings ('Thn' TLN 110; 'Eau:' 750; 'Pacis' 1374, etc.), and turned letters ('*clo[c]ke*' 1509, etc.). The compositors' botched work is evident from the use of lower-case type at the beginning of a speech (324, 424, etc.) and of speech-prefixes (717–20, etc.), the omission of punctuation marks after a speech (763, 903, etc.), after stage directions (444, 446, etc.), and after speech-prefixes (41, 463, 465, etc.). The paper used to print the Bodleian copy easily creased, sometimes affecting the text's readings. This caused the locally imperfect impression of type (41–2, 989, 1196–8). A couple of ink smudges can be seen at 11 and 431–2, the latter seriously affecting the text. Pressure from the press produced raised inked spaces and quads (the catchword on A2^v, 771, 1075, 1399–400, 1497), an extremely heavy impression (1061, etc.), and a number of instances of show-through. Show-through, usually caused either by thinner, poor-quality paper or by locally heavy inking, is visible in the running-titles on sigs C2^r, D4^r, E2^r, for example, and is less clearly noticeable in the blank space of 712 on C3^v, where part of 'Are' (675) on C3^r can be seen. Other instances are visible at 1170, 1177, 1180–1, and on E2^v, and are especially abundant on F1^r–F2^r.

The running-titles, or headlines, first appear on sigs A2^v–A3^r. They were composed in large roman type (with x-height of 3 millimetres) and read 'The tragicall History of' on versos and 'Doctor Faustus.' on rectos. There are no spelling variants. Examination of the Bodleian copy revealed several damaged types that were clear enough to identify eight separate running-titles. It is worth noting that the compositor (X) saved time and labour by re-using 'Doctor Faustus.' in the head-title (HT) on A2^r as the running-title on B2^r.[41]

---

[40] See TLN 479, 627, 631, 637, 897, 999, 1018, 1060, 1090, 1095, 1152, 1184, 1214, 1226, 1366, 1373, 1491, and 1515.

[41] It is less likely that 'Faustus.' used on the title-page was transferred to sig. B1^r for re-use, although type damage of its first 'u' does not look dissimilar. The stop in 'Faustus.' on B1^r is, however, roman, whereas that on the title-page is black-letter.

The arrangement of the eight running-titles by formes is as follows:[42]

Sheet	1[r]	2[v]	3[r]	4[v]	1[v]	2[r]	3[v]	4[r]
A	[t.p.]	a	b	c	–	d (HT)	e	f
B	g	a	b	c	h	d	e	f
C	b	c	g	a	h	d	e	f
D	b	c	g	a	h	d	e	f
E	d	h	f	e	c	b	a	g
F	b	c	g	–	h	d	–	–

The eight running-titles were regularly arranged to form two 'sets': Set I comprising 'a', 'b', 'c', and 'g', and Set II with 'd', 'e', 'f', and 'h'.[43] Both of the sets were used repeatedly in all sheets. Set I was used in the outer forme of sheets A–D and F and in the inner forme of sheet E, while Set II was employed in the inner forme of sheets A–D and F and in the outer forme of sheet E. When a book was printed in quarto a single set of the four running-titles formed part of the skeleton forme, accompanied by wooden furniture and quoins for locking up four quarto pages. In relation to standard procedures between imposition and press-work, the use of only one skeleton for both outer and inner formes was suitable for the operation of a single press, although this method prevented continuous press-work and wasted time, since the skeleton had to be transferred from one forme to the other. The use of two skeleton formes for the printing of Q1 could suggest that Simmes might have used two presses. There is, however, no evidence that he ever owned a second press. Although Simmes 'generally used one pair of skeletons for his books, and sometimes a single skeleton', W. Craig Ferguson conjectures that he had only one press, since his printing-house was 'a rather small establishment'.[44] Using two skeletons for one press, the compositors arranged for the outer forme to be imposed and printed with the Set I skeleton and the inner forme with the Set II skeleton, although they were exceptionally transposed in sheet E.[45]

---

[42] The identification of the running-titles coincides with that of Robert Ford Welsh in his 'The Printing of the Early Editions of Marlowe's Plays' (unpublished doctoral dissertation, Duke University, NC, 1964), pp. 109–10.

[43] Typographical discriminants of the eight running-titles are as follows: 'a' (lower-right serif of 'T' missing); 'b' (upper-right serif of the second 'u' broken); 'c' (upper-left serif of 'H' broken [not visible on sigs A4[v] and B4[v]] and tail of 'g' clearly connects with its link); 'd' (both upper and lower parts of bowl of 'D' cracked); 'e' (upper-left serif of 'H' broken like running-title 'c' but tail of 'g' detached from its link); 'f' (lower arm serif of 'F' broken and left sheared terminal of 'ct' ligature missing); 'g' (both upper-left and lower serifs of the first 'u' cracked); and 'h' (stem of 't' cracked and hooked terminal of the first 'a' broken). For the technical terms of types, see Philip Gaskell, 'A Nomenclature for the Letter-forms of Roman Type', *The Library*, 5th ser., 29 (1974), 42–51.

[44] Ferguson, *Valentine Simmes*, p. 81.

[45] For accounts of the use of two skeletons with one press, see Fredson T. Bowers, 'Notes on Running-Titles as Bibliographical Evidence', *The Library*, 4th ser., 19 (1938–9), 315–38, pp. 324–5.

Examination of the watermarks, using the unique copy, revealed that two kinds of watermark, a 'hand' and a 'pot', are visible in sheets A–F.[46] The hand watermark ('Ferguson 79', hereafter H) is visible in sheets A–E, while the pot watermark ('Ferguson 78', hereafter P) appears only in sheet F.[47] Neither watermark can be identified in standard reference sources, including digital watermark databases.[48] Ferguson made clear that H and P were two of as many as 108 watermarks that he could sketch from the copies of books available to him. On the basis of the large number of watermarks, it is evident that Simmes used a variety of cheap 'job-lots' of paper; this was not uncommon in the London printing-houses of the time.[49] Ferguson's list also indicates that P is one of only eight relatively common watermarks that recur in Simmes's books for three to five consecutive years: all the rest were short-lived and were discontinued within two years.

Sheet F of the surviving copy was no doubt thinner and inferior in quality compared with sheets A–E, for there are many instances of show-through in sheet F, as mentioned above. This is visible in almost all the page-area, including the headlines on sigs F1^r–F2^r.[50] At the time Q1 was published, the paper in general use in London was imported from the Continent, including Normandy and other parts of northern and central France, where such watermark designs as a 'Hand', a 'Pot', and 'Grapes' were favoured.[51] It seems likely, therefore, that the Bodleian copy of Q1 was printed with two kinds of paper of French origin.

---

[46] The marks are visible in the middle of the spine fold of conjugate leaves 1 and 4 (sheets A–B, D, F), or of leaves 2 and 3 (sheets C, E). I was unable to sketch the lower half of a pot that should have been visible on leaf F4, as it is lacking in the copy. Ferguson supplied the entire image from other sources (see n. 47 below).

[47] Ferguson sketched watermarks from all his accessible copies of books printed by Simmes in 1594–1611, in his *Valentine Simmes*, pp. 65–74. My research was conducted independently, and the result was consistent with his findings. He did not record, however, the watermark's distribution by sheet, nor did he identify the country of origin of the paper used for the Q1 copy. In terms of description of the marks' design, H would be classified as 'Hand with a quarter foil' and P as 'Pot with two handles and initials GB'.

[48] The reference works include Edward Heawood, *Watermarks: Mainly of the 17th and 18th Centuries* (Hilversum, 1950; repr. 1957); W. A. Churchill, *Watermarks in Paper in Holland, England, France, etc., in the XVII and XVIII Centuries and their Interconnection* (Amsterdam, 1935); C. M. Briquet, *Les Filigranes: dictionnaire historique des marques du papier dès leur apparition vers 1282 jusqu'en 1600*, 4 vols (Geneva, 1907; repr. New York, 1966). Searchable digital databases include 'The Thomas L. Gravell Watermark Archive' (http://www.gravell.org/); David L. Gants's 'A Digital Catalogue of Watermarks and Type Ornaments Used by William Stansby in the Printing of *The Workes of Beniamin Jonson* (London: 1616)' (http://www2.iath.virginia.edu/gants/); 'A Catalog of Paperstocks in The Shakespearian Pavier Quartos (1619)' by R. Carter Hailey (http://bsuva.org/bsuva/quartos/); 'The Watermark Database of the Dutch University Institute for Art History' (http://www.wm-portal.net/niki/index.php).

[49] For an account of the mixing of papers gathered by paper merchants, not by watermark but by size, see Allan H. Stevenson, 'Watermarks Are Twins', *Studies in Bibliography*, 4 (1951–2), 57–91, pp. 58–60. Ferguson's research reveals that the book that boasts the largest variety of watermarks (fifteen different 'Pots') was Michel de Montaigne's *The Essays* (1603; STC 18041) translated by John Florio.

[50] No show-through is visible on F3^r, since F3^v is blank.

[51] Heawood, *Watermarks*, pp. 24, 26.

Compositor identification was first undertaken by Robert Ford Welsh.[52] Welsh identified two compositors, X and Y, with the help of such distinguishing spellings as double '-ll' and single '-l' endings ('will' [X]/'wil' [Y], etc.), medial 'ea/ee' spellings ('year' [X]/'yeer' [Y], etc.), and the pronoun 'hee' [X] and 'he' [Y]. He also noticed that X normally sets *Exit/Exeunt* directions beginning with an upper-case initial letter, while Y prefers *exit/exeunt* with a lower-case initial letter. The division of their labour was also apparent, he contended, from a combination of speech-prefixes and punctuation marks that follow them: X favoured abbreviated speech-prefixes, punctuated with a stop, while Y preferred abbreviated speech-prefixes with a colon or unabbreviated speech-prefixes with no punctuation marks. Finally, Welsh identified the two compositors' stints throughout all pages with only twenty lines or so of text attributed with less confidence, due to equivocal or conflicting evidence. His compositor analysis was generally accepted by Fredson Bowers, and was later reviewed by Eric Rasmussen, who refined Welsh's results and confirmed the two compositors' stints with further evidence of their habitual practices.[53] The two compositors' stints revised by Rasmussen, with the location at the end of each stint, are as follows:

Compositor X		Compositor Y	
A2ʳ–B2ʳ	[end of page/speech]	B2ᵛ–B3ʳ	[end of page/speech]
(TLN 11–328)		(TLN 329–402)	
B3ᵛ	[end of page/speech]	B4ʳ–B4ᵛ36	[almost end of page/speech]
(TLN 403–37)		(TLN 438–510)	
B4ᵛ37–C2ʳ24	[after entry SD]	C2ʳ25–C3ʳ27	[end of speech]
(TLN 511–606)		(TLN 607–82)	
C3ʳ28–C3ᵛ30	[before entry SD]	C3ᵛ31–C4ᵛ15	[**middle** of prose]
(TLN 683–722)		(TLN 723–81)	
C4ᵛ16–37	[**middle** of prose; end of page]		
(TLN 782–803)			
D1ʳ28–D3ʳ8	[after exit SD]	D1ʳ1–27	[after exit SD]
(TLN 831–957)		(TLN 804–30)	
E2ʳ12–E3ʳ5	[after exeunt SD]	D3ʳ9–E2ʳ11	[before exit SD]
(TLN 1177–236)		(TLN 958–1176)	
E3ᵛ29–E4ᵛ11	[end of speech]	E3ʳ6–E3ᵛ28	[end of speech]
(TLN 1294–345)		(TLN 1237–93)	
F1ᵛ6–36	[end of page/speech]	E4ᵛ12–F1ᵛ5	[end of speech]
(TLN 1410–40)		(TLN 1346–409)	
		F2ʳ–F3ʳ	[end of page]
		(TLN 1441–528)	

---

[52] Welsh, 'The Printing of the Early Editions', pp. 86–126.

[53] *The Complete Works of Christopher Marlowe*, ed. Fredson Bowers, 2nd edn, 2 vols (Cambridge, 1981), 2.145–6; Eric Rasmussen, *A Textual Companion to 'Doctor Faustus'* (Manchester, 1993), pp. 18–24, 98–9. Rasmussen added 'bloud' [X]/'blood' [Y] to the spelling discriminators and revised part of Welsh's compositor attribution, especially that of sheet F.

It is notable that, whereas in sheets A–B and sigs F1ᵛ–F3ʳ almost every stint ends at the end of a page, the stints in sheets C–E and F1ʳ do not. The fact indicates, as Bowers observed, that the two sets of stints were undertaken in two distinct ways. Since each of the four stints from A2ʳ to B4ᵛ36 was finished precisely at the end of a page (except for a single line B4ᵛ37), this suggests that the text in sheets A–B (and F) was cast-off and X and Y set it by formes. On the other hand, in sheets C–E, the compositors finished their work at intermediate points such as either before or after a stage direction, at the end of a speech, or even in the middle of a prose speech. This change indicates that the compositors set the text in C–E seriatim. They mostly finished their work at what may have been a visibly prominent point in the manuscript; when there were no such obvious markers available, they stopped even in the middle of the prose text, such as on C4ᵛ15.[54] The reason for this switch from setting by formes to setting seriatim probably lies in the fact that sheets C–E contain a large number of prose speeches that overflow a full line. In contrast to verse speeches, long prose speeches would have made the compositors' calculations for the casting-off difficult and imprecise. The number of text-lines set as prose by sheet is 117 lines (sheet C), 130 (D), and 145 (E), while sheets A (two lines), B (94), and F (48) have far less prose text.[55] The compositors would have been assisted in casting-off the prose speeches in sheets B and F, because they appear in clusters on B1ʳ (twenty-four lines), B3ʳ (24), B3ᵛ (25), F1ᵛ (29), and F2ʳ (16). The rest of the pages in B contain only twenty-one lines of prose in all (there is no prose on B2ʳ and B2ᵛ), and in the remaining F pages there are a mere three prose lines (all verse on F2ᵛ and F3ʳ). In sheets C–E, however, the prose speeches are present on all pages except C1ʳ, E4ʳ, and E4ᵛ. It was therefore natural for X and Y to choose setting by formes for the first two and final sheets, but to switch to seriatim setting for the intermediate sheets in order to avoid having too little or too much text to set due to miscalculated casting-off.

In composing the text, X and Y probably did not work simultaneously using two separate type-cases. It is known that in 1604 Simmes possessed only a single pica black-letter fount.[56] The number of *STC* items for which Simmes printed the main text with black-letter founts of any size per year had shrunk rapidly since 1599; one in 1599, five each in 1600–1, two in 1602, and four in 1603, as against approximately thirty-five between 1594 (when Simmes started his business) and 1598. By contrast, he printed at least 116 items in roman in 1594–1604. In these circumstances, it is highly unlikely that Simmes decided to acquire more than a single case of pica black-letter shortly before and during 1604, and no bibliographical evidence suggests that X and Y would have used

---

[54] Marlowe, *Complete Works*, ed. Bowers, 2.146–7. Bowers suggested that 'the copy was not an easy one to cast off', but did not provide reasons for this. Welsh also conjectured that sheets C–E were set seriatim, based on the weaker evidence of type-shortage and the shifting of the skeleton formes in sheet E ('The Printing of the Early Editions', pp. 107–15).

[55] The counts do not include short prose speeches of less than a full line, since the compositors would not have had serious difficulties in casting them off.

[56] Ferguson, *Valentine Simmes*, p. 45.

two separate cases independently.⁵⁷ It is, therefore, almost certain that the two compositors were engaged in their work successively, not concurrently, using a single case.⁵⁸

Bushell was a London bookseller with a small business. While he was active during 1599–1618, he had fewer than thirty *STC* items printed for him, including Nicholas Breton's verse *Pasquil's Mad-Cap* (1600; STC 3675–5.5), Thomas Middleton's *Micro-Cynicon* (1599; STC 17154), and his *The Ant and the Nightingale* (1604; STC 17874.3). Apart from these, his books mainly (but not exclusively) comprise tracts and ephemeral pamphlets, with the result that *Faustus* was the only play he published throughout his career. Bushell, son of a Norwich tailor, was apprenticed to Nicholas Ling during 1591–9.⁵⁹ Ling was a publisher and bookseller in London (1580–5, 1590–1607) and Norwich (1585–90?), and had a close business relationship with Simmes. Simmes was commissioned to print about a third of Ling's books.⁶⁰ They were probably acquainted with each other during their years of apprenticeship to Henry Bynneman.⁶¹ Bushell may perhaps have procured the manuscript of *Faustus* with the help of his master. Ling seems to have some connections with the theatre, for he was the publisher of Q1 and Q2 *Hamlet* (1603, STC 22275; 1604, STC 22276). From the outset of his business career in 1599, Bushell frequently employed Simmes as his printer, for Simmes was his master's old friend and business partner: out of eighteen *STC* items that Bushell published before the end of 1604, twelve were printed by Simmes. Bushell would certainly have known that a year before he published Q1 *Faustus* Ling and Simmes had cooperated in producing Q1 *Hamlet*. Bushell's high esteem for Simmes may have led him to hire Simmes as the printer of Q1 *Faustus*.

Simmes's printing business was on a larger scale, with 'about 230 titles or editions' printed by him during 1594–1612.⁶² He is known to have printed a wide range of literary works, both classic and contemporary, including books written by Ariosto, Plutarch, Henry Chettle, Thomas Nashe, and, above all, Michel de Montaigne's literary landmark, *The Essays* (1603, STC 18041). He was also a renowned printer of a host of contemporary plays, including some

---

⁵⁷ Unfortunately, the type-recurrence evidence meticulously researched by Rasmussen does not sustain the theory that Simmes possessed a second case. Of all forty-two type-recurrences identified in X's and Y's stints, eighteen types (42.9%) do not reappear in the same compositor's later stint (Rasmussen, *Textual Companion*, pp. 100–3).

⁵⁸ The exact reason for the apparently inefficient employment of two compositors alternately using a single case is unknown. One can speculate that the division of labour may have been partly linked to their weekly wages.

⁵⁹ Arber, *Transcript*, 2.173, 723.

⁶⁰ Ferguson, *Valentine Simmes*, p. 26.

⁶¹ Ferguson, *Valentine Simmes*, p. 5. Ling was apprenticed to Bynneman during 1579–9. Although Simmes was, during 1577–85, an apprentice to Henry Sutton, a bookseller who ceased printing in 1562, he started to learn the work of composition at Bynneman's printing-house during his apprenticeship years.

⁶² W. Craig Ferguson, 'Valentine Simmes', in *The British Literary Book Trade, 1475–1700*, ed. James K. Bracken and Joel Silver, *Dictionary of Literary Biography*, 170 (Detroit, MI, 1996), 244–8, p. 244. Since as many as sixty imprints have his name alone (p. 245), he was also a publishing-printer.

by John Marston, George Chapman, Dekker, Thomas Heywood, and, most notably, Shakespeare: Q1 *Richard III* (1597; STC 22314), Q1–3 *Richard II* (1597–8; STC 22307–9), Q1 *Much Ado About Nothing* (1600; STC 22304), Q1 *2 Henry IV* (1600; STC 22288–8a), and Q4 *1 Henry IV* (1604; STC 22282). Simmes's business was flourishing in 1604:[63] in addition to Q4 *1 Henry IV*, he printed Dekker's *The Honest Whore* (1604; STC 6501), three editions of Marston's *The Malcontent* (1604; STC 17479–81), Ben Jonson's *King James his Royal and Magnificent Entertainment* (1604; STC 14756), and William Alexander's closet dramas, *The Monarchic Tragedies* (1604; STC 343). Like most of his fellow stationers, he was constantly at risk of offending against the rules of the Company and, in one case in 1607, he fell foul of the authorities to the extent that he was stripped of his status as a master printer. Nevertheless, he was a competent printer 'certainly at or above the standard of the day'.[64] It is evident that Q1 was one of the plays Simmes produced while he was undoubtedly busy, but he had sufficient experience and expertise in the craft to cope with the demands of producing a dramatic text.

The Play's Source and Early History

There is a general consensus about the main source of the play: the *Historia von D. Johann Fausten* (commonly called the *Faustbuch*). This book, which provided Marlowe with a wide range of materials for the composition of almost all the scenes, was a prose collection of the anecdotes, events, and incidents relating to Faustus. It was originally written in German and was published in Frankfurt am Main in 1587. Marlowe used its English translation by 'P.F. *Gent.*', *The History of the Damnable Life and Deserved Death of Doctor John Faustus* (1592; STC 10711), which is widely known as the 'English Faust Book' (EFB).[65] Although the 1592 EFB once served as the basis for the claim of '1592–3' as the date of the play, it was actually a reprint.[66] Since 2001,

---

[63] Ferguson *Valentine Simmes*, p. 22, states that 1604 was his second busiest year after 1596.

[64] The nature of his offence is unknown. See *Records of the Court of the Stationers' Company 1602 to 1640*, ed. William A. Jackson (London, 1957), p. 24, and Ferguson, 'Valentine Simmes', p. 248.

[65] There is no evidence that the German original was translated into Latin. John Henry Jones identified Paul Fairfax as 'the most promising candidate' for the role of translator, in his edition of *The English Faust Book: A Critical Edition Based on the Text of 1592* (Cambridge, 1994), pp. 11–34, p. 33. Fairfax, a German-speaking traveller in Eastern Europe who claimed to have received a doctorate from Frankfurt, was reported to have sold in London pamphlets advertising 'Aqua Coelestis' (heavenly water). He practised his medical treatment with this distilled water and pills, for which the Royal College of Physicians fined him £5 in 1588. See 'Physicians and Irregular Medical Practitioners in London 1550–1640' (https://www.british-history.ac.uk/no-series/london-physicians/1550-1640/fairfax-paul), accessed 17 March 2018.

[66] The 1592 EFB was 'Newly imprinted, and in conueni-|ent places imperfect matter amended.'. The only complete copy survives in the British Library; a single sheet of sig. A survives at Shrewsbury School, but this 'Shrewsbury fragment' belongs, according to Jones, not to the 1592 EFB, as *STC* and ESTC state, but was printed early in 1592 before the 1592 EFB was published (*English Faust Book*, pp. 34–52).

discoveries of documentary evidence suggesting the existence of a hitherto unknown 'Pre-1592' edition of the EFB have moved the date back to '1588' or '1589'.[67] This earlier EFB has, it seems, provided a firm basis on which to determine the play's date. It also seems likely that Gabriel Harvey's reference to 'an other Doctour Faustus, threateneth to coniure-vpp at leysure', in part of a book dated 5 November 1589, relates to the 'Pre-1592' EFB.[68] The key to determining a more exact date for the EFB would be the ballad version of the Faustus story. On 28 February 1589, 'A ballad of the life and deathe of Doctor Faustus the great Cunngerer' was entered by Richard Jones, but no copy of the ballad survives.[69] The close similarity of the ballad title to the 1592 EFB and to Edward Barlow's catalogue entry suggests that the ballad was probably based on EFB.[70] The publication of the ballad version probably reflects the growing popularity of the Faustus story, for, as John Henry Jones argued, 'the balladeer commonly traded on established public awareness of the plot material', for example, of 'recent, sensational events, such as notorious murders or daring escapades of war', and they provided, in the form of ballads, 'a popular and entertaining gloss' on them. On the basis of the fact that ballad-makers and their publishers were keenly aware that 'The topical interest for such subjects guaranteed sales', Jones rightly concluded that 'it is most unlikely that a ballad of Doctor Faustus would have been published until public interest had been awakened'.[71] In line with his argument, to posit a period of a month or two would be appropriate before London citizens became ready to amuse themselves with the ballad of Faustus, either directly by reading EFB or through widespread gossip about it. It is, then, reasonable to conjecture that copies of EFB were available to London citizens in January or early February 1589.

[67] See R. J. Fehrenbach, 'A Pre-1592 English Faust Book and the Date of Marlowe's *Doctor Faustus*', *The Library*, 7th ser., 2 (2001), 327–35. 'Doctor faustus' was recorded in a probate inventory, compiled in 'late November 1589' (p. 334), of Matthew Parkin, an Oxford scholar who died that year. It is 'listed in the midst of English translations' (p. 331). Another EFB, 'Doctor faustus lief & deathe', was found entered in a private book catalogue compiled in 1590 by Edward Barlow (fl. 1571–94), a London apothecary and grocer; see *Private Libraries in Renaissance England: A Collection and Catalogue of Tudor and Early Stuart Book-Lists*, ed. R. J. Fehrenbach and E. S. Leedham-Green, 9 vols (Tempe, AZ, 1992–2017), 6.242–3, 250; 9.45–7, 74. See also the Database 'PLRE. Folger' (http://plre.folger.edu/). I am grateful to Professor Fehrenbach for providing me with information on Barlow's book catalogue.

[68] The reference occurs in Harvey's '*An Aduertisement for Pap-hatchet, and Martin Marprelate*', which is dated at its end, 'At Trinitie hall: this fift of Nouember: 1589.', and was later brought into print as part of *Pierce's Supererogation* (1593; STC 12903), sigs I4r–S3v, R3r. See Paul H. Kocher, 'The Early Date for Marlowe's *Faustus*', *Modern Language Notes*, 58 (1943), 539–42.

[69] Greg, *Parallel Texts*, p. 6; Arber, *Transcript*, 2.516.

[70] In his 'Three Old Ballads and the Date of "Doctor Faustus"', *Journal of the Australasian Universities Language and Literature Association*, 36 (1971), 187–200, MacDonald P. Jackson conjectured that Jones's ballad was transcribed in 1609–16 to become one of the Shirburn ballads, and concluded that the ballad derived directly from the play. But the Shirburn ballad's title, 'The Judgment of God shewed vpon *Jhon Faustus*, Doctor of Divinitye', is different from that of the ballad Jones entered. This identification cannot be certain, unless a copy of Jones's ballad is discovered. For the Shirburn ballads, see *The Shirburn Ballads 1585–1616*, ed. Andrew Clark (Oxford, 1907), pp. 72–5.

[71] Jones, *English Faust Book*, p. 54.

There are some further contemporary references to 'Faustus' that support the earlier date of the play's composition. According to Paul H. Kocher, Thomas Nashe's marginalia left on his copy of John Leland's *Principum, ac illustrium aliquot & eruditorum in Anglia virorum, encomia* (1589; STC 15447) directly allude to the play.[72] 'Faustus: Che sara sara deuinynitie adieu' is Nashe's obvious recollection of Faustus's speech in Q1, 'Che sera, sera, | What wil be, shall be? Diuinitie, adieu,' (TLN 87–8). When he repeated 'deuiyntninie adieu' again on another page,[73] Nashe also jotted down there, 'Faustus: studie in indian silke', an allusion to Faustus's 'Ile haue them fill the publike schooles with silk. | Wherewith the students shalbe brauely clad:' (cf. TLN 132–3).[74] Nashe only once referred to Leland and the book's editor, Thomas Newton. This was in the preface, addressed to the gentlemen students of Oxford and Cambridge, to Robert Greene's *Menaphon* (1589; STC 12272, on sig. A1r), which was entered in the Stationers' Registers on 23 August 1589. Kocher argued that Nashe may have purchased and read the collection of Latin poems shortly after its publication and soon after mentioned Leland and Newton in his contribution to Greene's book.[75] It is tempting to think that Nashe somehow had a chance to be involved in the play, either by watching a performance or writing its comic scenes in collaboration with Marlowe. Too much weight, however, should not be placed on his brief jottings in his copy of *Principum*, since they are undated.

Harvey also left undated marginalia in one of his books. On a page of Richard Morysine's translation of Sextus Julius Frontinus' *The Stratagems, Sleights, and Policies of War* (1539; STC 11402), Harvey wrote 'if Doctor Faustus cowld reare Castles, & arme Diuels at pleasure'. This is believed to have been inscribed in 1589–90 and is regarded as deriving not from EFB but directly from the tragedy, although there is no decisive evidence for this.[76] Another possible echo of Faustus in the late 1580s is, again, subject to interpretation. In his *Perimedes the Black-Smith* (1588; STC 12295), Greene mentioned 'such mad and scoffing poets […] as bred of *Merlins* race […] that set the end of scollarisme in an English blanck verse' (sig. A3r-v). The key phrases '*Merlins* race' and 'the end of scollarisme' may perhaps refer to Faustus's

---

[72] Paul H. Kocher, 'Some Nashe Marginalia Concerning Marlowe', *Modern Language Notes*, 57 (1942), 45–9. The book comprises Leland's Latin poems edited by Thomas Newton, followed by Newton's own poems in Latin.

[73] Kocher wondered if Nashe was punning on the word 'ninny' in the two instances of 'deuinynitie' and 'deuiyntninie' (p. 46, n.5).

[74] Alexander Dyce's emendation in *The Works of Christopher Marlowe*, 3 vols (London, 1850), 2.10, of the original text's 'skill' to 'silk' has been widely accepted.

[75] Kocher, 'Some Nashe Marginalia', pp. 48–9.

[76] Hale Moore, 'Gabriel Harvey's References to Marlowe', *Studies in Philology*, 23 (1926), 337–57. Moore states that Harvey 'would certainly have heard of the play on the London stage, even though he did not see it in person' (p. 348). Harvey's copy of Frontinus is at Harvard University (Harvard, STC 11402); the annotation occurs on sig. G7r.

'Diuinitie, adieu' speech mentioned above.[77] But the 1592 EFB also has it that Faustus 'beleeued not that there was a God [...] and had quite forgotten Diuinitie' (B2ᵛ). If it were possible to demonstrate that Greene was remembering Faustus on stage, then it could be shown that the play existed by the end of 1588 (or, allowing for the legal year, by 25 March 1589 at the latest).[78] Finally, if it is agreed that, in view of their stylistic similarities, the composition of *Faustus* followed immediately after *2 Tamburlaine*, *Faustus* might have been composed in 1588, for both *1* and *2 Tamburlaine* were performed 'before the end of 1587'.[79] The most recent scholarship on contemporary references to both EFB and *Faustus* suggests that the earliest date of the play falls between 1588 and 1589. Martin Wiggins announced in 2012 that his 'Best Guess' was '1588', while his 'Limits' were '1587–9'.[80]

Anonymous manuscript notes inscribed on the final page of an unnamed title printed by Thomas Vautrollier in 1585 reported that a devil appeared on the stage while 'Certaine Players at Exeter acting *upon* the stage the tragicall storie of Dr. Faustus the Conjurer [...] (as I heard it)'.[81] If this theatrical event actually happened in the West Country, it might be the earliest reference to the play being performed in 1588–9 or the early 1590s. Some critics used to argue that *Faustus* was performed at the Theatre that existed in Shoreditch between 1576 and 1597, on the grounds that Thomas Middleton's *The Black Book* (1604; STC 17875) mentions 'Diuells in Docter Faustus, when the olde Theater crackt and frighted the Audience' (sig. B4ʳ). It is, however, not sufficiently clear what 'the olde Theater' actually refers to. It may have been the Rose, which would indeed have been deemed 'olde' after the Fortune was newly built in 1600, or the event described may possibly have been fictional.[82] William Prynne referred to a Faustus play in his *Histrio-Mastix* (1633; STC 20464–4a): 'many now alive, who well remember it' informed him that '*there being some distracted with that fearefull sight*' of the '*visible apparition of the Devill on the Stage at the Belsavage Play-house*' while '*the History of* Faustus' was performed (3G*4ʳ). The Bel Savage Inn, with open-air yards surrounded by a balcony, is known to have been used for the 'prize' fight by fencers from the 1570s, as well as for dramatic performances from 1576 until after 1588. E. K. Chambers suggested that the Admiral's Men might have played *Faustus*

---

[77] See Donna N. Murphy, 'The Date and Co-Authorship of *Doctor Faustus*', *Cahiers Élisabéthains*, 75 (2009), 43–4; Charles Whitney, *Early Responses to Renaissance Drama* (Cambridge, 2006), p. 176. Murphy (p. 44) and Whitney conjecture with 'probably' and 'perhaps', respectively.

[78] On 29 March 1588, Edward White, the publisher of *Perimedes*, was required to secure licence and authorization for the book before printing it (Arber, *Transcript*, 2.488).

[79] E. K. Chambers, 'The Date of Marlowe's *Tamburlaine*', *Times Literary Supplement*, 28 August 1930, p. 684. See also Wiggins, *British Drama*, 2.375, 378, 385, 389.

[80] Wiggins, *British Drama*, 2.419.

[81] Under the heading 'Minor Correspondence', this was reported by one 'J. G. R', in *The Gentleman's Magazine*, September 1850, p. 234.

[82] See Eric Rasmussen, '*The Black Book* and the Date of *Doctor Faustus*', *Notes and Queries*, 235 (1990), 168–70; Wiggins, *British Drama*, 2.426. Rasmussen states that the reference originates from an invented story of Faustus and has nothing in common with Marlowe's tragedy (p. 169).

there, as Prynne's anecdote indicates.[83] Shortly after Marlowe's death in 1593, George Peele paid tribute to him in *The Honour of the Garter* ([1593]; STC 19539): 'vnhappy in thine end, | *Marley*, [...] Fitte to write passions for the soules below' (*A*2ᵛ). Peele may perhaps have alluded to the underworld depicted in *Faustus*, although it is not evidently clear.[84] By the time Marlowe's death was widely known, the Faustus legend seems to have been prevalent in the minds of London citizens and contemporary authors. In the year following, an anonymous writer naming himself an 'English Gentleman Student' published a Faust story-book, *The Second Report of Doctor John Faustus Containing his Appearances and the Deeds of Wagner* (1594; STC 10715–5.3).

The earliest London performance of the play recorded in Philip Henslowe's 'diary' dates from 30 September 1594 and is no doubt a revival. It was acted by the Admiral's Men at the Rose, with the protagonist played by the company's leading actor, Edward Alleyn, who had married Henslowe's step-daughter. Alleyn is said to have appeared on stage 'With a crosse vpon his breast'.[85] Henslowe, the theatre manager, recorded a total of twenty-five performances up to and including 13 October 1597.[86]

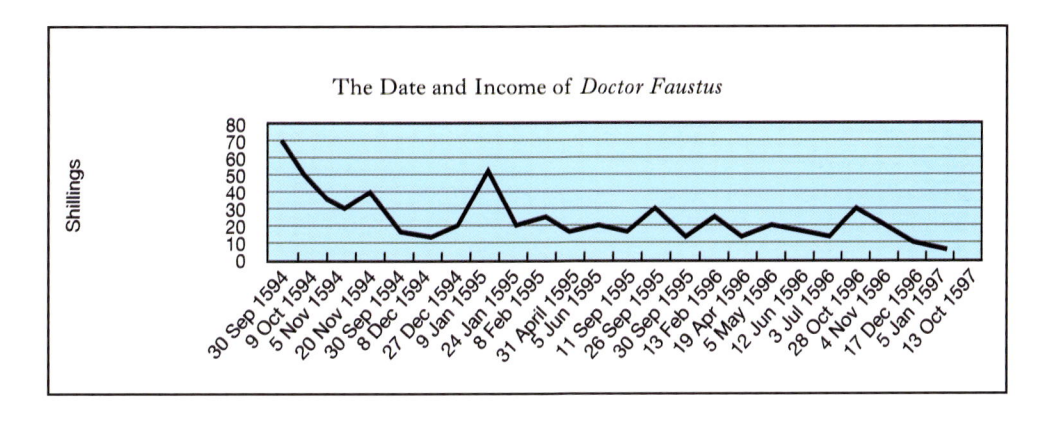

Faustus, one of the Admiral's Men's most popular plays, achieved its highest revenue, 72*s.*, on the first day of its revival, 30 September 1594. This suggests that the audience, already familiar with the play, found nothing attractive in the subsequent performances so that they did not frequently revisit the theatre. The revenue taken then indicates that, since Henslowe's income represents

---

[83] E. K. Chambers, *The Elizabethan Stage*, 4 vols (Oxford, 1923), 2.382.
[84] Whitney, *Early Responses to Renaissance Drama*, p. 176.
[85] Samuel Rowlands, *The Knave of Clubs* (1609; STC 21387), sig. D3ʳ. The book was originally entered on 2 September 1600.
[86] *Henslowe's Diary*, ed. R. A. Foakes, 2nd edn (Cambridge, 2002), pp. 24–8, 30–1, 34, 36, 47, 54–5, 60. Henslowe's income on 13 October 1597 cannot be ascertained from his manuscript (p. 60).

'half the takings from the galleries',[87] there were at least 864 spectators, if they had each paid two pence to sit in the gallery. Afterwards, Henslowe's income from the play steadily diminished, with the exception of the 1594 Christmas performance (27 December) with 52s. While the play was acted at least twice a month between October 1594 and January 1595, only five performances were recorded from February 1595 to the end of that year. From mid-1596, income fell sharply to less than 20s. (excepting 28 October), and reached only 9s. before Christmas (17 December). On 5 January 1597, the play recorded its lowest-ever earnings, 5s., that is, 7 per cent of its highest takings. This indicates that the audience sitting in the gallery numbered only sixty. Observing the radical downturn in the play's popularity, Henslowe decided to halt its staging after 13 October 1597.

During 1594–7, *The Wise Man of West Chester* (now lost) formed, with *Faustus*, a pair of the Admiral's marketable items, with the former as 'a comedic complement to the demonic wizardry' of the latter.[88] On the other hand, the same period almost precisely corresponds with the years during which Thomas Kyd's *The Spanish Tragedy* (performed 1592–3, 1597) ceased being staged.[89] Complementing each other, *Faustus* and *The Spanish Tragedy* obviously formed the representative, although somewhat outdated, plays of the Admiral's during 1592–7. It is interesting to note that in the inventory of the Admiral's goods (March–April 1598) are 'j Hell mought', 'the sittie of Rome', 'j dragon in fostes', and 'a robe for to goo invisibell'. There also can be found 'faustus Jerkin his clok' in the list of the company's playing apparel (c.1602).[90] Once very popular and enormously successful, the two tragedies had lost their theatrical appeal by late 1597 after a good many performances with a more-or-less overused theatrical playbook (promptbook), although some small-scale revisions, including topical allusions or improvised gags, may have been added from time to time by actors different from the original cast. In 1601–2, Henslowe commissioned some of his dramatists, including Dekker, Heywood, and Jonson, to refresh plays in poor demand by supplying additional passages.[91] This implies that by 1601 Henslowe had given up staging them, and that they were stored in his warehouse. It is known that Alleyn, who had temporarily retired between

---

[87] Andrew Gurr, *Shakespeare's Opposites: The Admiral's Company, 1594–1625* (Cambridge, 2009), p. 201.

[88] Roslyn L. Knutson, 'Play Identifications: *The Wise Man of West Chester* and *John a Kent and John a Cumber*; *Longshanks* and *Edward I*', *Huntington Library Quarterly*, 47 (1984), 1–11, p. 7. *The Wise Man* was performed intermittently from 2 December 1594 to 18 July 1597. See Martin Wiggins with Catherine Richardson, *British Drama 1533–1642: A Catalogue: Volume III: 1590–1597* (Oxford, 2013), p. 259.

[89] *The Spanish Tragedy* had been performed sixteen times between 14 March 1592 and 22 January 1593, and after four years' hiatus, there were thirteen performances between 7 January 1597 and 11 October 1597. See Wiggins, *British Drama*, 2.373.

[90] See Foakes, *Henslowe's Diary*, pp. 319–20, 325, 293, respectively.

[91] Henslowe's payments for additions were to Jonson for *The Spanish Tragedy* on 25 September 1601 and 22 June 1602, to William Birde and Samuel Rowley for *Faustus* on 22 November 1602; other payments were to Dekker for *Oldcastle* and to Heywood for *Cutting Dick*. See Foakes, *Henslowe's Diary*, pp. 182, 203, 206, 213, 216.

1597 and 1600, returned to the stage in 1601. It was only then that Henslowe determined to revive the plays with revised texts.[92]

Baron Waldstein, a young Czech undergraduate at Strasbourg University, began a diary on 1 January 1597, soon after his matriculation. He left a note of ten plays that he saw performed at Strasbourg by a troupe of English actors in July and August 1597.[93] On 12 August he saw 'Comoediae […] de Fausto', a Faustus play now widely identified as Marlowe's.[94] The troupe was led by Thomas Sackville, who from 1592 had gained popularity as a clown in Germany. Since he was mentioned in his passport signed and issued by Charles Howard, the Lord Admiral, as one of his 'joueurs et serviteursis' (players and servants),[95] Sackville may also have acted at the Rose as one of the clowns before 1592. In the same year, 1597, that Waldstein saw the Faustus play, Faustus was referred to by Edward Sharpham (bap. 1576, d. 1608), playwright and pamphleteer. He briefly mentioned that 'Mephostophilus neuer haunted D. Faustus more' (sig. E1r) in his *The Discovery of the Knights of the Post* (1597; STC 21489).

The Printer's Manuscript of the Play

Scholars generally believe that the play's comic scenes were not composed by Marlowe (who never wrote a comedy) but by a collaborator who has yet to be identified. Nashe is a likely candidate at present, in view of the fact that his works share a number of verbal parallels and recurring rare words with Marlowe.[96] As mentioned above, Nashe also left curious marginalia about the play in his copy of Leland's *Principum* inscribed, probably, in 1589. On the other hand, the common vocabulary and rare words aside, Ruth Stevenson has argued that the play's 'buffoonery outweighs [Nashe's] sharp satire' in most of the comic scenes, and that 'the semantic and syntactic density of Nashe's prose seems unlike the slapstick flare-ups and simple, jagged vocabulary' in them.[97] Based on the analysis of function words, Rasmussen discussed the division of Q1's authorship between Marlowe and the collaborator.[98] He suggested that the collaborator may have been Henry Porter, Marlowe's Cambridge contemporary and the author of *1 The Two Angry Women of Abingdon* (1599; STC 20121.5,

---

[92] For the events that follow and the revision of *Faustus*, see the introduction to *Doctor Faustus 1616*.

[93] See *The Diary of Baron Waldstein: A Traveller in Elizabethan England*, tr. and ed. G. W. Groos (London, 1981), pp. 10–11.

[94] Willem Schrickx, *Foreign Envoys and Travelling Players in the Age of Shakespeare and Jonson* (Gent, 1986), p. 330.

[95] J. G. Riewald, 'New Light on the English Actors in the Netherlands, c. 1590–c. 1660', *English Studies*, 41 (1960), 65–92, p. 71; Schrickx, *Foreign Envoys*, pp. 195–8.

[96] *Doctor Faustus: A- and B-texts (1604, 1616)*, ed. David Bevington and Eric Rasmussen (Manchester, 1993), p. 72.

[97] Ruth Stevenson, 'The Comic Core of Both A- and B-Editions of *Doctor Faustus*', *Studies in English Literature, 1500–1900*, 53 (2013), 401–19, p. 402.

[98] See Rasmussen, *Textual Companion*, pp. 62–75.

20122), first performed by the Admiral's (Nottingham's) Men perhaps in 1598. Word-frequency tests are, it has recently been argued, unreliable when applied to small segments of a work, such as Q1's comic episodes or chorus scenes. Even the relatively long comic Scene 9 of the Knight and the Horse-courser episode (TLN 1048–275) has fewer than 1,900 words of dialogue. To make a reasonably valid case, the most recent computerized authorship analysis requires a segmented text of 'typically 2,000 words', while 'the minimal sample length varied from 2,500 words (Latin prose) to 5,000 or so words' (English poems and novels).[99] For the time being, perhaps until further investigation clears up the problem, the long-standing conjecture that the A-text was written by Marlowe and an unknown collaborator is all that can be definitely stated.

Q1 has only 1,518 lines of main text. According to Alfred Hart, the average length of 204 plays written between 1590 and 1616 is 2,447 lines (except for Ben Jonson's).[100] This means that the A-text is only 62 per cent of the average length, although it falls outside the period that Hart investigated. In the middle of the twentieth century, its exceptional brevity formed one of the reasons for supposing that the text had been reproduced from the players' memories.[101] As the 'memorial reconstruction' theory gradually fell out of favour in the 1990s,[102] Rasmussen argued, mainly from textual duplication, that the printer's copy was Marlowe's and his collaborator's 'foul papers', interleaved with other manuscript material.[103] In the 'double ending' passage (TLN 1022–47), Mephistopheles enters, '*sets squibs*' at the back of Robin, Rafe, and Vintner to surprise them, re-enters, and transforms the three to animals. Immediately after this slapstick action, however, Mephistopheles curses them anew, discloses that he came far off from Constantinople, and transforms the two clowns (only) into animals once again. With reference to other instances in Q2 *Romeo and Juliet* (1599; STC 22323) in support of the 'foul papers' origin of the printer's copy of Q1 *Faustus*, Rasmussen concluded that the compositor (Y), unable to understand the author's deletion mark, accidentally set both the cancelled and revised texts.[104]

---

[99] Hugh Craig and Brett Greatley-Hirsch, *Style, Computers, and Early Modern Drama: Beyond Authorship* (Cambridge, 2017), p. 30, and Maciej Eder, 'Does Size Matter? Authorship Attribution, Small Samples, Big Problem', *Digital Scholarship in the Humanities*, 30 (2015), 167–82, pp. 161, 171–2, respectively.

[100] Alfred Hart, 'Acting Versions of Elizabethan Plays', *The Review of English Studies*, 10 (1934), 1–28, p. 4. Since Jonson's plays are 'abnormally long, averaging nearly 3,580 lines', they were excluded from Hart's computations; see also his 'The Length of Elizabethan and Jacobean Plays' and 'The Time Allotted for Representation of Elizabethan and Jacobean Plays', *The Review of English Studies*, 8 (1932), 139–54, p. 153, 395–413.

[101] Leo Kirschbaum, 'The Good and Bad Quartos of *Doctor Faustus*', *The Library*, 4th ser., 26 (1945–6), 272–94; Greg, *Parallel Texts*, pp. 29–62.

[102] See especially Laurie E. Maguire, *Shakespearean Suspect Texts: The 'Bad' Quartos and Their Contexts* (Cambridge, 1996); Paul Werstine, 'A Century of "Bad" Shakespeare Quartos', *Shakespeare Quarterly*, 50 (1999), 310–33.

[103] Rasmussen, *Textual Companion*, pp. 14–17.

[104] In Q2 *Romeo*, Romeo and Friar Laurence repeat 'The grey eyde morne' speech in nearly identical manner (sig. D4ᵛ). Duplication of this kind has been regarded as Shakespeare's second thoughts. See also Romeo's duplicated dying speeches on L3ʳ.

Although such textual duplication also occurs in *Sir Thomas More*, written by the hands of multiple authors, it is, in fact, not unique to authorial 'foul papers'. John Clavell's *The Soldered Citizen* (*c*.1628–31), a transcribed playhouse manuscript, presents the same phenomenon.[105] According to Paul Werstine, of five duplicated passages, four instances were clearly crossed out, leaving no possibility of being misunderstood. However, in the middle of a stanza of a song, the first version is left standing with a reference mark (X) placed at the beginning of line 3, while two lines of the second version are written in the right-hand margin with the same reference mark at the beginning, thereby representing the revised lines 3–4. The bookkeeper of *The Soldered Citizen*, Edward Knight of the King's Men, did not insert a prominent deletion mark here, such as a large cross, a bracket, or a long vertical stroke, all of which can be seen in *More*. The fact that, although he left a reference mark, Knight never crossed out the original version, as he did with the four other instances, would suggest that he probably envisaged plural textual authority. In other words, he felt no difficulty in keeping both the original and revised texts, as if to archive them for future use on different occasions.[106] The duplication left in Q1 *Faustus* may have resulted from one of the following two cases. Compositor Y, unable to decipher the bookkeeper's handwritten mark, may have set both versions of the speeches. As Werstine argued, the 'sheer variety of ways used by playhouse personnel to indicate deletion may well have confused printers and may account for reproduction of duplicate passages in print'.[107] Alternatively, the bookkeeper may have intended to keep both passages. As Constance Brown Kuriyama argued, the duplicated passages in Q1 may have been two alternative versions depending on 'the availability of the squibs' or on their effectiveness with different audiences. The first version simply aims at slapstick, while the second 'emphasizes character and verbal humor'.[108] During the long run of the play's performances, an audience tired of the bustling comic scene might have preferred the revised passage, perhaps presented by a different cast of comedians.

It seems hard to credit that Marlowe and the collaborator's original manuscript still survived, even in part, fifteen or so years after the original play's composition. As Blayney put it, 'Manuscripts written for practical use do not last forever', and the theatrical playbook of *King Lear* 'might need to be replaced more than once in seventeen years'.[109] Once the *Faustus* playbook was complete, the 'foul papers' would have been discarded. The printer's copy

---

[105] For the date of the play, see Martin Wiggins with Catherine Richardson, *British Drama 1533–1642: A Catalogue: Volume VIII: 1624–1631* (Oxford, 2017), p. 468.

[106] Paul Werstine, *Early Modern Playhouse Manuscripts and the Editing of Shakespeare* (Cambridge, 2012), pp. 188–90.

[107] Werstine, *Early Modern Playhouse Manuscripts*, p. 188.

[108] Constance Brown Kuriyama, 'Review of *Doctor Faustus: A- and B-texts (1604, 1616)* edited by David Bevington and Eric Rasmussen', *Medieval and Renaissance Drama in England*, 8 (1996), 241–9, p. 246.

[109] Peter W. M. Blayney, 'Quadrat Demonstrandum', *Papers of the Bibliographical Society of America*, 111 (2017), 61–101, p. 95.

of Q1 was probably not the authors' papers, but a manuscript originating in the theatre. As has already been mentioned, the stage direction '*exit Meph.*' (TLN 1252) is printed *within* a speech by Faustus. The bookkeeper may have emphasized in the playbook that Mephistopheles had to exit (and re-enter '*with the grapes*' at 1253–4) while Faustus was still speaking. Moreover, Q1 has some traces indicating revisions added in the theatre after the play's original composition. The permissive '*et cetera*' in Robin's speech, 'I scorne you: and you are but a &c.' (TLN 1005–6), is a sign for the actor's embellished improvisation, as Kuriyama pointed out.[110] The '&c' in the speech would have been filled with a vulgar word or an allusive phrase that may have been different in almost every performance. This device was obviously something actors, especially popular comedians, favoured to please the audience. It seems unlikely that Marlowe's collaborator, responsible for the comic scene, had it in mind from the beginning. The reviser or the bookkeeper may have added it in a later theatrical revision as required. In addition, the reference to Dr Roderigo Lopez indicates a theatrical addition originating from the 1594 performance. The Horse-courser's cry, 'mas Doctor Lopus was neuer such a Doctor' (TLN 1186–7), was clearly a topical allusion to the Queen's Portuguese-Jewish physician executed for treason on 7 June 1594.[111] His scandalous death on the scaffold at Tyburn was such a striking event that, in the following November, William Cecil, Lord Burghley, published a pamphlet describing the deadly plots contrived by Lopez and others, making details of their treason well known among London citizens.[112] Under the circumstances, the play's topical allusion could have been devised by the actor and added to the playbook by the bookkeeper at some point between June 1594, when Lopez was hanged, and 30 September 1594, when the Admiral's Men revived the play. Alternatively, it may have been added shortly after the pamphlet's publication in November 1594.

The name of the dramatic company given on Q1's title-page, '*the Right Honorable the Earle of Nottingham his seruants*', was in use only for a brief span of six years, from 22 October 1597 when their patron Charles Howard was created Earl of Nottingham, until about Christmas 1603, when the company entered Prince Henry's service.[113] Ten first editions of plays, including Q1 *Faustus*, have a title-page indicating the company's affiliation to Nottingham. They were all published during 1598–1604.[114] Significantly, excepting Q1

---

[110] Kuriyama, 'Review of *Doctor Faustus*', p. 245. For instances of similar kinds of 'ad libbing', see Tiffany Stern, *Documents of Performance in Early Modern England* (Cambridge, 2009), pp. 250–1.

[111] Edgar Samuel, 'Lopez [Lopes], Roderigo [Ruy, Roger] (*c.*1517–1594)', *ODNB*, accessed 17 March 2018.

[112] William Cecil, *A True Report of Sundry Horrible Conspiracies* (1594; STC 7603–3 5). The title-page of STC 7603 indicates that it was published in 'Nouember.'.

[113] Chambers, *Elizabethan Stage*, 2.186.

[114] The ten plays comprise Chapman's *The Blind Beggar of Alexandria* (1598), *An Humorous Day's Mirth* (1599), Porter's *The Two Angry Women of Abingdon* (1599), Dekker's *Old Fortunatus* (1600), *The Shoemakers' Holiday* (1600), *1 Sir John Oldcastle* (1600), Munday's *The Downfall of Robert Earl of Huntingdon* (1601), *The Death of Robert Earl of Huntingdon* (1601), Dekker's *Patient Grissel* (1603), and *Faustus* (1604).

Faustus (1604), the plays are all known to have been performed, at least once, during the years that the company was officially entitled Nottingham's.[115] This means that their title-pages provided the correct designation for their acting company. It is evident that, so far as these nine plays are concerned, the publishers were careful enough not to give incorrect information to their buyers. This fact in turn suggests that Bushell may well have known that *Faustus* was also performed by Nottingham's Men after 22 October 1597. Since Q1's date of publication falls outside the six years that the company was called Nottingham's, Bushell correctly sought to inform readers that the play was performed, at least once, by Nottingham's Men.[116] It is, therefore, more than probable that the performance of the play continued even after 13 October 1597 when Henslowe's extant records end.

The Admiral's Men's performances from September 1594 to October 1597 were apparently not sufficiently successful to keep drawing large audiences, although they often supplied a small increase in Henslowe's income. It would have been essential for such a long-running, popular play as *Faustus* to be slightly updated during the three years of performances, so that Henslowe could satisfy both the audience and the management of the Rose and its company. Although there is no hard evidence, it is tempting to suggest that, by October 1597, the 1594 playbook would have received minor textual changes by the actors/sharers, including the excision or the replacement of topical allusions or improvisations as well as substitutions in the cast. As a result, the outdated playbook may have been replaced by a new one, freshly transcribed by the bookkeeper.[117] Alternatively, it is likely that, some time after 22 October 1597, Nottingham's Men, on receiving their new title, altered the 1594 playbook to initiate their new title with a new playbook. If either of these inferences is correct, there was no problem for the Admiral's/Nottingham's Men in releasing the obsolescent script to a stationer. On the basis of the fact that the permissive '&c' and the allusion to Dr Lopez are present in Q1, the manuscript that Bushell acquired for printing was probably the Admiral's Men's 1594 playbook. The available evidence from Q1's title-page and its text suggests that, in 1601, Bushell entered the Admiral's outdated 1594 playbook version of *Faustus* in the Stationers' Registers and, three years later, published Q1 with the title-page indicating the name of the acting company responsible for the play's performances. Although it is more than likely that Nottingham's Men kept on performing it for some time after 1597, the tragedy's life had

---

[115] See Wiggins, *British Drama*, 3.328 (*Blind Beggar*), 390 (*Humorous Day's Mirth*); Martin Wiggins with Catherine Richardson, *British Drama 1533–1642: A Catalogue: Volume IV: 1598–1602* (Oxford, 2014), pp. 12 (*Downfall of Robert*), 17 (*Death of Robert*), 72, 89 (*Two Angry Women*), 116 (*Shoemakers' Holiday*), 156 (*Oldcastle*), 171 (*Old Forunatus*), 198 (*Patient Grissel*).

[116] John Wright, the publisher of Q2 and Q3 *Faustus* (1609 and 1611) did not include the company's name on the title-page of these editions; his reprinted editions of *The Shoemakers' Holiday* (1610, 1618, 1624, 1631, 1657) retained the name of the original acting company.

[117] This type of alteration may have caused the sudden upsurge in Henslowe's income in December 1594. The three performances on 8, 20, and 27 December yielded 15s., 18s., and 52s., respectively. The revenue that Henslowe received from the Christmas performance on 27 December marked the second highest peak of all his recorded income, as described above.

almost come to an end. In 1602, Henslowe decided to lease the existing playbook to William Birde and Samuel Rowley in preparation for extensive revisions and additions in accordance with changes in the audience's tastes. *Faustus* needed a full-scale transformation.

The Bodleian Copy of the 1604 Quarto

The Bodleian copy of Q1 once belonged to Edmond Malone (1741–1812), the Shakespearean scholar, editor, and commentator. Rebound in 'quarter brown goatskin over cloth boards' in April 1929, it was one of 'just short of a thousand early printed plays' bequeathed to the Bodleian Library in Oxford. Malone's collection of plays included those that George Steevens (1736–1800), attracted by the younger man's great promise as a scholar, generously gave him in 1778, as well as the plays that Malone himself acquired.[118] Malone also owned a copy of Q9 *Faustus* (1631; STC 17436), along with a copy of each of Marlowe's six other plays published in the late sixteenth and the early seventeenth centuries.[119] Shortly after Malone's death, his elder brother, Richard Malone (1738–1816), Baron Sunderlin of Baronston, arranged for Malone's books and literary papers to be used by James Boswell, Junior, who was then preparing his variorum edition. In 1815, Richard Malone decided to bequeath the bulk of his brother's library to the Bodleian, for he was well aware of 'the high and just respect which he [Edmond] felt for the university of Oxford, and the sense that he entertained of the politeness and liberality which he always met with from that body in his researches'.[120] Malone's books and papers were finally sent to Oxford by the younger Boswell in 1821 when he had completed his twenty-one volume variorum edition of *The Plays and Poems of William Shakespeare*.[121]

Opposite the title-page of his copy of Q1, Malone left an autograph memorandum in heavy brown ink describing Q1's brief publication history as well as some notes on the play's later additions (see Appendix for a transcript). After adding his handwritten initials 'E.M.' (l. 22),[122] he went on to cast doubt on Q1's status as the first edition in view of the 1601 entrance in the

---

[118] Stephen Hebron, *Marks of Genius: Masterpieces from the Collections of the Bodleian Libraries* (Oxford, 2014), p. 339; James M. Osborn, 'Edmond Malone: Scholar-Collector', *The Library*, 5th ser., 19 (1964), 11–37, p. 12.

[119] His library included O1 of *1 & 2 Tamburlaine* (1590; STC 17425), Q1 of *Dido* (1594; STC 17441), O1 of *The Massacre at Paris* ([1594?]; STC 17423), Q2 and Q4 of *Edward II* (1598, STC 17438; 1622, STC 17440), Q1 of *1 Tamburlaine* (1605; STC 17428), and Q1 of *Jew of Malta* (1633; STC 17412). See *Catalogue of Early English Poetry and other Miscellaneous Works Illustrating the British Drama, Collected by Edmond Malone, Esq. and Now Preserved in the Bodleian Library* (Oxford, 1836), p. 24.

[120] For a transcript of Richard's letter to the Vice-Chancellor of Oxford University of 7 July 1815, see *Catalogue of Early English Poetry Collected by Edmond Malone*, p. ii.

[121] Peter Martin, *Edmond Malone, Shakespearean Scholar: A Literary Biography* (Cambridge, 1995), pp. 277–9.

[122] Malone's signature can also be seen both on the endpaper opposite the title-page and on the verso of the title-page (mounted) of the Bodleian copy of Shakespeare's *Richard III* (1612; STC 22318, Arch. G d.39 (6)).

Stationers' Registers, recording his suspicions at the foot of the page. As he was, presumably, not content with this, he rewrote his thoughts as a postscript at the head of the page. He meticulously paid more attention to details of the entrance by adding the name of the copy-holder and a more precise date when the play was entered. Finally, he reached the conclusion (though erroneously) that there probably existed a 1601 edition preceding Q1. A 1601 copy has yet to be discovered, nor is existing scholarship able to give a full account of the three years' gap between Bushell's entrance and Q1's publication.[123]

There are two handwritten inscriptions on the title-page, a minuscule 'f' in the right-hand outer margin and the numeral '6' at the top right-hand corner. Although they appear to be written in brown ink similar to Malone's, it is not at all clear whether they were inscribed either by Malone himself or by an earlier owner. It is hard to know exactly what the minuscule 'f' stands for, but it does not look very dissimilar to what George M. Kahrl calls 'a large sweeping f', a marking that 'appears on books in Dulwich College Library which came originally from William Cartwright' (1606–86), the actor, publisher, and collector. Kahrl states that David Garrick's four copies of plays, with a curved 'f' written in ink on their title-page, originate from the Cartwright Collection. Three of the four copies aside, the mark on *The Tragedy of Antigone* (1631; STC 17716, BL shelfmark 643.b.36) looks similar to that inscribed on the title-page of Q1 *Faustus*. This alone, however, does not constitute evidence that Malone's copy had once belonged to Cartwright.[124] The numeral '6' perhaps indicates one of the sequential numbers attached to several titles that were once bound together into a single volume. There are also some blots and indecipherable marks in brown ink in the text, including what appears to be an exclamation mark (TLN 21) and an ink blot affecting the text (365).[125]

It is known that Sir John Harington (bap. 1560, d. 1612), Queen Elizabeth's godson, the renowned translator of Ludovico Ariosto's *Orlando Furioso* and an enthusiastic collector of plays, possessed a copy of *Faustus*. In his manuscript list of some 135 English printed plays appears 'Doctor Faustus' as one of thirteen plays rebound together in a single volume, two others of which were Marlowe's quarto editions of *1 Tamburlaine* (1605; STC 17428) and *2 Tamburlaine* (1606; STC 17428a). Unfortunately, it is impossible to decide with certainty whether his copy of 'Doctor Faustus' was Q1 or Q2 (1609), for the list was 'drawn up in the winter of 1609–10'.[126] One of three surviving copies of Q2 is now held at Petworth House in Petworth, West Sussex, home of the Percy family, earls of

---

[123] Coincidentally, Alleyn returned to the stage in 1601, the year of Bushell's entrance, while 1604 was the year when Alleyn finally left the Fortune.

[124] George M. Kahrl with Dorothy Anderson, *The Garrick Collection of Old English Plays: A Catalogue with an Historical Introduction* (London, 1982), pp. 18, 143 (no. 434), 282–3. I am grateful to Tanya Kirk, Lead Curator of the British Library, for providing information on the four BL copies.

[125] Brown ink blots and marks can also be seen at TLN 115 (outer margin), 275, and 319 (outer margin).

[126] Greg, *Bibliography*, 3.1307. For Greg's transcript of the entire catalogue, inscribed on a single folio leaf (fol. 43) of British Library Add. MS 27632, and his accounts of it, see his *Bibliography*, 3.1306–13.

Northumberland for centuries from the Middle Ages. The Petworth collection contains 149 English plays printed between 1585 and 1638, and was assembled by William Percy (1574–1648), a poet and amateur dramatist. A friend at Oxford of Barnabe Barnes, who published *The Devil's Charter* (1607; STC 1466–6a), Percy left six manuscript plays including *The Cuckqueans and Cuckolds Errants* (1601) in three Percy collections now held at Alnwick Castle and the Henry E. Huntington Library.[127] Percy's copy of Q2 (NT 3007510), rebound with other titles in a single volume with sprinkled calf and red sprinkled edges, has a gilt centrepiece on both covers that shows 'crescent moon, surrounded by garter motto with earl's coronet on top', the Percy arms. It also contains a 'Manuscript volume contents list in a seventeenth-century hand'.[128] The Huntington Library holds a single copy each of Q2 and Q3.[129] The Q2 copy (Call Number 62486) once belonged to the Bridgewater Library. The collection, started in about 1600 by Sir Thomas Egerton (1540–1617), first Viscount Brackley and Lord Chancellor, was 'probably the oldest large family library in the United Kingdom'. Rare books, literary manuscripts, and family papers were sold en bloc to Henry E. Huntington in 1917. On the upper right-hand corner of the copy's title-page is a handwritten numeral '9.' surrounded by three lines forming a square, open at the top, the mark characteristic of the Bridgewater collection.[130] The Huntington copy of Q3 (62485) is the only surviving exemplar of the 1611 edition.[131] It was one of the books in the Chatsworth Library collected by the dukes of Devonshire from the early eighteenth century. It has the bookplate of Spencer Compton Cavendish (1833–1908), politician and the eighth duke.[132] In 1914, it was decided that the Caxtons and the plays from the Chatsworth Library were to be sold; they were bought by Huntington.[133]

*

[127] See Edward Miller, 'A Collection of Elizabethan and Jacobean Plays at Petworth', *The National Trust Year Book 1975–76* (1975), pp. 62–4; Harold N. Hillebrand, 'William Percy: An Elizabethan Amateur', *Huntington Library Quarterly*, 1 (1937–8), 391–416; George F. Reynolds, 'William Percy and His Plays, with a Summary of the Customs of Elizabethan Staging', *Modern Philology*, 12 (1914–15), 241–60.

[128] See the copy's 'Bibliographic description' in the 'National Trust Collection' database (http://www.nationaltrustcollections.org.uk/), accessed 10 September 2017. The Petworth copy has the final blank leaf (sig. F4).

[129] The Huntington copy of Q2 lacks the final blank leaf. A third copy of Q2 is held in Hamburg Staats- und Universitätsbibliothek; it has the final blank leaf.

[130] Seymour de Ricci, *English Collectors of Books & Manuscripts (1530–1930) and Their Marks of Ownership* (Cambridge, 1930), pp. 17–19.

[131] The copy lacks sig. A1. The chain-lines of the paper on which it is printed run vertically, because the paper used by the printer (George Eld) for this copy was in extra-large size and had to be torn in half to print a quarto volume. As a result, the chain-lines appear to be vertical as against the horizontal lines in paper of normal size. For this phenomenon, see Gaskell, *New Introduction*, p. 84.

[132] For bibliographical information on both Q2 and Q3 copies, see the 'Huntington Library Catalog' (http://catalog.huntington.org/), accessed 10 September 2017.

[133] De Ricci, *English Collectors*, pp. 78–81.

The present photographic facsimile comprises a 1:1 full-colour reproduction of the unique copy of Q1 in the Bodleian Library, Oxford, with, as an Appendix, Malone's autograph inscriptions on an upper endpaper.[134]

The inner margins provide 'Through Line Numbers', beginning with the title on sig. A1ʳ. Catchwords are not included in the count.

---

[134] Malone's inscriptions are reproduced in poor photographic quality in 'EEBO', but not in an earlier collotype reproduction, *The Tragicall History of D. Faustus*, Tudor Facsimile Texts, ed. John S. Farmer (Amersham, Bucks., 1914), or in a xerographic edition, Christopher Marlowe, *Doctor Faustus 1604 and 1616*, Scolar Press Facsimile (Menston, 1970). Most recently, Hebron's *Marks of Genius*, p. 338, provided a reduced photographic image in full colour.

P.S. Enterd in the Stationers Regr. by
T. Bushell, Jany 7. 1600-1. Probably
therefore there was an edn. in 1601.

The original edition; at least no
earlier is now known.—
This is Marlowe's original play,
of which I was not possessed when
I formed my general collection, of his works in
one large volume bound in red
morocco. Large additions were
made to this play by Wm. Bird and
Samuel Rowley in Nov. 1602. See
my History of the English Stage p.320.
edit. 1790. Marlow had then
been above nine years dead;
and his play, tho' very popular
remained unpublished. On its revival & these additions being
made, the possessor of the copy a
copy of the original was induced
to commit it to the press. it
indeed this was the first edn. [?]
which I doubt, for it was entered in the Stationers
by Bushell in [?]

APPENDIX

Edmond Malone's Manuscript Notes on Q1 *Faustus*[1]

In this transcript, the original layout and line divisions are reproduced. Malone wrote his postscript at the head of the page. The published *Catalogue* of Malone's collection says nothing about Marlowe's 'one large volume bound in red morocco' (ll. 9–10). Malone's reference to 'History of the English Stage p. 320, edit. 1790' (13–14) is to the 'Emendations and Additions' following 'An Historical Account of the Rise and Progress of the English Stage', in *The Plays and Poems of William Shakspeare*, ed. Edmond Malone, 10 vols (1790), I [part 2], p. 320, where Malone transcribed Henslowe's payment to Birde and Rowley for their additions recorded on 22 November 1602.

P S. Entered in the Stationers Reg^r. by
T.Bushell, Jany 7, 1600–1 – Probably
therefore there was an ed^n in 1601.

    The original edition, at least no
earlier is now known. ——
    This is Marlowes original play,
of which I was not possessed when
I formed my general Collection \of his works/ in
one large volume bound in red
morocco.. Large additions were   10
made to this play by W^m. Bird and
Samuel Rowley in Nov. 1602. See
my History of the English Stage p. 320,
edit. 1790. Marlowe had then
been above nine years dead;
and his play, tho' very popular
remained unpublished. On its re
vival & these additions being
made, the possessor of [the ori] a
copy of the original was induced   20
to commit it to the press.
if indeed this was the first editn. E.M.
[of] which I doubt, for it was entered in the Stat^{rs} Reg^r
      by Bushell in Jan^y \1600–1601./

8 of his works] interlined above caret   9 bound] *o* blotted   12 Samuel] *m* blotted
17 unpublished] *sh* blotted   20 original] *na* blotted   24 1600–1601.] inserted in left-hand margin between and above carets

---

[1] This transcript follows standard Malone Society conventions: interlineations are enclosed within oblique lines \thus/. Deletions are enclosed within square brackets [thus]. I am grateful to H. R. Woudhuysen for checking my transcript. Responsibility for any remaining errors is, of course, mine.

LIST OF ROLES

(In order of their appearance in the 1604 quarto)

Chorus
Doctor Faustus, a scholar
Wagner, Faustus's servant
The Good Angel
The Evil Angel
Valdes, Faustus's friend
Cornelius, Faustus's friend
Two Scholars
Mephistopheles, a devil
Robin, the clown
Balliol, a devil
Belcher, a devil
Dancing devils attending Mephistopheles
A devil dressed as a woman
Lucifer, the principal devil
Beelzebub, a devil, Lucifer's companion
Pride
Covetousness
Wrath
Envy
Gluttony
Sloth
Lechery
The Pope
The Cardinal of Lorraine
Friars
Rafe, Robin's colleague
A Vintner
The Emperor of Germany
A Knight
Attendants on the Emperor
A spirit of Alexander the Great
A spirit of his Paramour
A Horse-Courser
The Duke of Anhalt
The Duchess of Anhalt
Three Scholars
A spirit of Helen of Troy
An Old Man
Devils

OBSCURED AND DAMAGED READINGS

The following list consists of readings containing broken, blotted, or uninked letters and punctuation; turned letters (mostly 'u' and 'n', but at TLN 1509 '*clocke*' with ²*c* turned) have not been recorded. Roman and black-letter readings are represented in roman. Each missing piece of type or blank space is represented by a point between angle brackets. In the case of TLN 431, no attempt has been made to estimate how many missing characters or spaces there might be where it has proved impossible to determine their number—Greg, *Parallel Texts*, p. 186, notes that Q1 may read '*possibly* any thing', which is Q2's reading. The 'Full' readings have been verified against Greg's *Parallel Texts*.

TLN	Visible Reading	Full Reading
31	s<.>lfe	selfe
71	*hæred<.>tari*	*hæreditari*
	n<.>n	*non*
74	<.>is	His
97	commaun<.>	commaund
106	*V*alde<.>	*V*aldes
	Corneliu<.>	Cornelius
150	wit<.>	wits
183	<.>ath	Hath
190	entrail<.>s	entrailes
193	magi<.>all	magicall
208	<.>le	Ile
357	<.>s	as
362	Aff<.>icke	Affricke
389	<.>eft	left
431	a< >g	anything
440	Ba<.>ioll	Balioll
506	pe<.>petual	perpetual
569	on<.>t	on't
654	B<.>	Be
734	will <.>	will I
797	thith<.>r	thither
825	b<.>	by
862	groundwor<.>e	groundworke
922	bl<.>ate	bleate
951	wondr<.>d	wondred
959	admirabl<.>! h<.>re	admirable! here
1011	hon<.>st	honest
1031	th<.>one	th'one
1084	vs<.>e	vsde
1090	I<.>aith	Ifaith
1092	<.>efore	before

xliii

1231	<.>agner	Wagner
1262	Indi<.>	India
1438	co<.>e	come
1440	migh<.> <.>aue prayed for t<.>ee?	might haue prayed for thee?
1464	<.>ime	time
1484	<.>atiuitie	natiuitie

THE TRAGICALL

History of D. Faustus.

As it hath bene Acted by the Right Honorable the Earle of Nottingham his seruants.

Written by Ch. Marl.

LONDON
Printed by V.S. for Thomas Bushell. 1604.

The tragicall Historie
of Doctor Faustus.

Enter Chorus.

Not marching now in fields of Thracimene,
Where Mars did mate the Carthaginians,
Nor sporting in the dalliance of loue,
In courts of kings where state is ouerturnd,
Nor in the pompe of prowd audacious déedes,
Intends our Muse to daunt his heauenly verse:
Onely this (Gentlemen) we must performe,
The forme of Faustus fortunes good or bad.
To patient Judgements we appeale our plaude,
And speake for Faustus in his infancie:
Now is he borne, his parents base of stocke,
In Germany, within a towne calld Rhodes:
Of riper yéeres to Wertenberg he went,
Whereas his kinsmen chiefly brought him vp,
So soone hée profites in Diuinitie,
The fruitfull plot of Scholerisme grac't,
That shortly he was grac't with Doctors name,
Excelling all, whose sweete delight disputes
In heauenly matters of Theologie,
Till swolne with cunning of a selfe conceit,
His waxen wings did mount aboue his reach,
And melting heauens conspirde his ouerthrow.
For falling to a diuelish exercise,
And glutted more with learnings golden gifts,

A 2   He

The tragicall History of

He surffets vpon cursed Negromancy,
Nothing so sweete as magicke is to him
Which he preferres before his chiefest blisse,
And this the man that in his study sits.   *Exit.*

Enter Faustus in his Study.

Faustus Settle thy studies Faustus, and beginne
To sound the deapth of that thou wilt professe:
Hauing commencde, be a Diuine in shew,
Yet leuell at the end of euery Art,
And liue and die in Aristotles workes:
Sweete Anulatikes tis thou hast rauisht me,
Bene disserere est finis logicis,
Is, to dispute well, Logickes chiefest end
Affords this Art no greater myracle:
Then reade no more, thou hast attaind the end:
A greater subiect fitteth Faustus wit,
Bid Oncaymæon farewell, Galen come:
Seeing, *vbi desinit philosophus, ibi incipit medicus.*
Be a physition Faustus, heape vp golde,
And be eternizde for some wondrous cure,
Summum bonum medicinæ sanitas,
The end of physicke is our bodies health:
Why Faustus, hast thou not attaind that end?
Is not thy common talke sound Aphorismes?
Are not thy billes hung vp as monuments,
Whereby whole Citties haue escapt the plague,
And thousand desprate maladies bœne easde,
Yet art thou still but Faustus, and a man.
Wouldst thou make man to liue eternally?
Or being dead, raise them to life againe?
Then this profession were to be esteemd.
Physicke farewell, where is Iustinian?
Si vna eademq́, res legatus duobus,
Alter rem alter valorem rei, &c.
A pretty case of paltry legacies:
Ex heredatari filium n̄n potest pater nisi
Such is the subiect of the institute

And

Doctor Faustus.

And vniuersall body of the Church:
His study fittes a mercenary drudge,
Who aimes at nothing but externall trash,
Too seruill and illiberall for me:
When all is done, Diuinitie is best.
Ieromes Bible, Faustus, view it well.
Stipendium peccati mors est: ha, *Stipendium*, &c.
The reward of sinne is death: thats hard.
Si peccasse negamus, fallimur, & nulla est in nobis veritas.
If we say that we haue no sinne,
We deceiue our selues, and theres no truth in vs.
Why then belike we must sinne,
And so consequently die.
I, we must die an euerlasting death:
What doctrine call you this, *Che sera, sera*,
What wil be, shall be? Diuinitie, adieu,
These Metaphisickes of Magicians,
And Negromantike bookes are heauenly
Lines, circles, sceanes, letters and characters:
I, these are those that Faustus most desires.
O what a world of profit and delight,
Of power, of honor, of omnipotence
Is promised to the studious Artizan?
All things that moue betweene the quiet poles
Shalbe at my commaund, Emperours and Kings,
Are but obeyd in their seuerall prouinces:
Nor can they raise the winde, or rend the cloudes:
But his dominion that excedes in this,
Stretcheth as farre as doth the minde of man.
A sound Magician is a mighty god:
Heere Faustus trie thy braines to gaine a deitie.

Enter Wagner.

Wagner, commend me to my dearest friends,
The Germaine Valdes, and Cornelius,
Request them earnestly to visite me.
  Wag. I wil sir.   *exit.*
  Fau. Their conference will be a greater help to me,

A 3   Than

The tragicall History of

Thn all my labours, plodde I nere so fast.

Enter the good Angell and the euill Angell.
Good. A. O Faustus, lay that damned booke aside,
And gaze not on it, lest it tempt thy soule,
And heape Gods heauy wrath vpon thy head,
Reade, reade the scriptures, that is blasphemy.
Euill An. Go forward Faustus in that famous art,
Wherein all natures treasury is contain'd:
Be thou on earth as Ioue is in the skie,
Lord and commaunder of these Elements. *Exeunt.*
Fau. How am I glutted with conceit of this?
Shall I make spirits fetch me what I please,
Resolue me of all ambiguities,
Performe what desperate enterprise I will?
Ile haue them flye to India for gold,
Ransacke the Ocean for orient pearle,
And search all corners of the new found world
For pleasant fruites and princely delicates:
Ile haue them reade mee straunge philosophie,
And tell the secrets of all forraine kings,
Ile haue them wall all Iermany with brasse,
And make swift Rhine circle faire Wertenberge,
Ile haue them fill the publike schooles with skill.
Wherewith the students shalbe brauely clad:
Ile leuy souldiers with the coyne they bring,
And chase the Prince of Parma from our land,
And raigne sole king of all our prouinces:
Yea stranger engines for the brunt of warre,
Then was the fiery keele at Antwarpes bridge,
Ile make my seruile spirits to inuent:
Come Germaine Valdes and Cornelius,
And make me blest with your sage conference,
Valdes, sweete Valdes, and Cornelius,

Enter Valdes and Cornelius.

Know that your words haue won me at the last,

To

Doctor Faustus.

To practise Magicke and concealed arts:
Yet not your words onely, but mine owne fantasie,
That will receiue no obiect for my head,
But ruminates on Negromantique skill,
Philosophy is odious and obscure,
Both Law and Phisicke are for pettie wits,
Diuinitie is basest of the three,
Vnpleasant, harsh, contemptible and vilde,
Tis Magicke, Magicke that hath rauisht mee,
Then gentle friends ayde me in this attempt,
And I that haue with Consistylogismes
Graueld the Pastors of the Germaine Church,
And made the flowring pride of Wertenberge
Swarme to my Problemes as the infernall spirits
On sweet Musæus when he came to hell,
Will be as cunning as Agrippa was,
Whose shadowes made all Europe honor him.

  Vald. Faustus these bookes thy wit and our experience
Shall make all nations to canonize vs,
As Indian Moores obey their Spanish Lords,
So shall the subiects of euery element
Be alwaies seruiceable to vs three,
Like Lyons shall they guard vs when we please,
Like Almaine Rutters with their horsemens staues,
Or Lapland Gyants trotting by our sides,
Sometimes like women, or vnwedded maides,
Shadowing more beautie in their ayrie browes,
Then in their white breasts of the quæne of Loue:
For Venice shall they dregge huge Argoces,
And from America the golden fleece,
That yearely stuffes olde Philips treasury
If learned Faustus will be resolute.

  Fau. Va'des as resolute am I in this
As thou to liue, therefore obiect it not.

  Corn. The myracles that Magicke will performe,
Will make thee vow to studie nothing else,
He that is grounded in Astrologie,

                          Inricht

The tragicall History of

Inricht with tongues, well seene minerals,
Hath all the principles Magicke doth require,
Then doubt not (Faustus) but to be renowmd,
And more frequented for this mystery,
Then heretofore the Delphian Oracle.
The spirits tell me they can drie the sea,
And fetch the treasure of all forraine wrackes,
I, all the wealth that our forefathers hid
Within the massie entrailes of the earth.
Then tell me Faustus, what shal we three want?

Fau. Nothing Cornelius, O this cheares my soule,
Come shewe me some demonstrations magicall,
That I may coniure in some lustie groue,
And haue these ioyes in full possession.

Val. Then haste thee to some solitary groue,
And beare wise Bacons and Albanus workes,
The Hebrew Psalter, and new Testament,
And whatsoeuer else is requisit
Wee will enforme thee ere our conference cease.

Cor. Valdes, first let him know the words of art,
And then all other ceremonies learnd,
Faustus may trie his cunning by himselfe.

Val. First Ile instruct thee in the rudiments,
And then wilt thou be perfecter then I.

Fau. Then come and dyne with me, and after meate
Weele canuas euery quidditie thereof:
For ere I sleepe, Ile trie what I can do,
This night Ile coniure though I die therefore.

Exeunt.

Enter two Schollers.

1. *Sch.* I wonder whats become of Faustus, that was wont to make our schooles ring with, *sic probo.*

2. *Sch.* That shall we know, for see here comes his boy.

Enter Wagner.

1. *Sch.* How now sirra, wheres thy maister?

Wag. God in heauen knowes.

2. Why, dost not thou know?

Wag.

Doctor Faustus.

Wag. Yes I know, but that followes not.

1. Go to sirra, leaue your ieasting, and tell vs where hée is.

Wag. That followes not necessary by force of argument, that you being licentiate should stand vpon't, therefore acknowledge your error, and be attentiue.

2. Why, didst thou not say thou knewst?

Wag. Haue you any witnesse on't?

1. Yes sirra, I heard you.

Wag. Aske my fellow if I be a thiefe.

2. Well, you will not tell vs.

Wag. Yes sir, I will tell you, yet if you were not dunces you would neuer aske me such a question, for is not he corpus naturale, and is not that mobile, then wherefore should you aske me such a question: but that I am by nature flegmaticke, slowe to wrath, and prone to leachery, (to loue I would say) it were not for you to come within fortie foote of the place of execution, although I do not doubt to sée you both hang'd the next Sessions. Thus hauing triumpht ouer you, I will set my countnance like a precisian, and begin to speake thus: truly my deare brethren, my maister is within at dinner with Valdes and Cornelius, as this wine if it could speake, it would enforme your worships, and so the Lord blesse you, preserue you, and kéepe you my deare brethren, my deare brethren.

exit.

1. Nay then I feare he is falne into that damned art, for which they two are infamous through the world.

2. Were he a stranger, and not alied to me, yet should I grieue for him: but come let vs go and informe the Rector, and sée if hée by his graue counsaile can reclaime him.

1. O but I feare me nothing can reclaime him.

2. Yet let vs trie what we can do.

Exeunt.

Enter Faustus to coniure.

Fau. Now that the gloomy shadow of the earth,
Longing to view Orions drisling looke,

B   Leapes

The tragicall History of

Leapes from th'antartike world vnto the skie,
And dimmes the welkin with her pitchy breath:
Faustus, begin thine incantations,
And trie if diuels will obey thy hest,
Seeing thou hast prayde and sacrifiz'd to them.
Within this circle is Iehouahs name,
Forward and backward, and Agramithist,
The breuiated names of holy Saints,
Figures of euery adiunct to the heauens,
And characters of signes and erring starres.
By which the spirits are inforst to rise,
Then feare not Faustus, but be resolute,
And trie the vttermost Magicke can performe.
*Sint mihi dei acherontis propity, valeat numen triplex Iehouæ, ignei,
aërÿ, Aquatani spiritus saluete, Orientis princeps Belsibub, inferni
ardentis monarcha & demigorgon, propitiamus vos, vt apariat &
surgat Mephastophilis, quod tumeraris, per Iehouam gehennam &
consecratam aquam quam nunc spargo, signúmque crucis quod nunc
facio, & per vota nostra ipse nunc surgat nobis dicatis Mephastophilis.*

Enter a Diuell.

I charge thee to returne and chãunge thy shape,
Thou art to vgly to attend on me,
Goe and returne an old Franciscan Frier,
That holy shape becomes a diuell best.　　　　*Exit diuell.*
I see theres vertue in my heauenly words,
Who would not be proficient in this art?
How pliant is this Mephastophilis?
Full of obedience and humilitie,
Such is the force of Magicke and my spels,
No Faustus, thou art Coniurer laureate
That canst commaund great Mephastophilis,
Quin regis Mephastophilis fratris imagine.

Enter Mephostophilis.

Me.　Now Faustus, what wouldst thou haue me do?
Fau.　I charge thee wait vpon me whilst I liue,

Doctor Faustus.

To do what euer Faustus shall commaund,
Be it to make the Moone drop from her spheare,
Or the Ocean to ouerwhelme the world.
 Me. I am a seruant to great Lucifer,
And may not follow thee without his leaue,
No more then he commaunds must we performe.
 Fau. Did not he charge thee to appeare to mee?
 Me. No, I came now hither of mine owne accord.
 Fau. Did not my coniuring speeches raise thee? speake.
 Me. That was the cause, but yet per accident,
For when we heare one racke the name of God,
Abiure the scriptures, and his Sauiour Christ,
Wee flye, in hope to get his glorious soule,
Nor will we come, vnlesse he vse such meanes
Whereby he is in danger to be damnd:
Therefore the shortest cut for coniuring
Is stoutly to abiure the Trinitie,
And pray deuoutly to the prince of hell.
 Fau. So Faustus hath already done, & holds this principle
There is no chiefe but onely Belsibub,
To whom Faustus doth dedicate himselfe,
This word damnation terrifies not him,
For he confounds hell in Elizium,
His ghost be with the olde Philosophers,
But leauing these vaine trifles of mens soules,
Tell me what is that Lucifer thy Lord?
 Me. Arch-regent and commaunder of all spirits.
 Fau. Was not that Lucifer an Angell once?
 Me. Yes Faustus, and most dearely lou'd of God.
 Fau. How comes it then that he is prince of diuels?
 Me. O by aspiring pride and insolence,
For which God threw him from the face of heauen.
 Fau. And what are you that liue with Lucifer?
 Me. Vnhappy spirits that fell with Lucifer,
Conspir'd against our God with Lucifer,
And are for euer damnd with Lucifer.
 Fau. Where are you damn'd?

B 2   Me.

The tragicall History of

Me. In hell.

Fau. How comes it then that thou art out of hel?

Me. Why this is hel, nor am I out of it:
Thinkst thou that I who saw the face of God,
And tasted the eternal ioyes of heauen,
Am not tormented with ten thousand hels,
In being depriu'd of euerlasting blisse:
O Faustus, leaue these friuolous demaunds,
Which strike a terror to my fainting soule.

Fau. What, is great Mephastophilis so passionate,
For being depriud of the ioyes of heauen?
Learne thou of Faustus manly fortitude,
And scorne those ioyes thou neuer shalt possesse.
Go beare those tidings to great Lucifer,
Seeing Faustus hath incurrd eternall death,
By desprate thoughts against Ioues deitie:
Say, he surrenders vp to him his soule,
So he will spare him 24. yeeres,
Letting him liue in al voluptuousnesse,
Hauing thee euer to attend on me,
To giue me whatsoeuer I shal aske,
To tel me whatsoeuer I demaund,
To slay mine enemies, and ayde my friends,
And alwayes be obedient to my wil:
Goe and returne to mighty Lucifer,
And meete mee in my study at midnight,
And then resolue me of thy maisters minde.

Me. I will Faustus.   *exit.*

Fau. Had I as many soules as there be starres,
Ide giue them al for Mephastophilis:
By him Ile be great Emprour of the world,
And make a bridge through the moouing ayre,
To passe the Ocean with a band of men,
Ile ioyne the hils that binde the Affricke shore,
And make that land continent to Spaine,
And both contributory to my crowne:
The Emprour shal not liue but by my leaue,

Doctor Faustus.

Nor any Potentate of Germany:
Now that I haue obtaind what I desire,
Ile liue in speculation of this Art,
Til Mephastophilis returne againe. *exit.*

Enter Wagner and the Clowne.

Wag. Sirra boy, come hither.

Clo. How, boy: swowns boy, I hope you haue seene many boyes with such pickadeuaunts as I haue. Boy quotha?

Wag. Tel me sirra, hast thou any commings in?

Clo. I, and goings out too, you may see else.

Wag. Alas poore slaue, see how pouerty iesteth in his nakednesse, the vilaine is bare, and out of seruice, and so hungry, that I know he would giue his soule to the Diuel for a shoulder of mutton, though it were bloud rawe.

Clo. How, my soule to the Diuel for a shoulder of mutton though twere bloud rawe? not so good friend, burladie I had neede haue it wel roasted, and good sawce to it, if I pay so deere.

Wag. wel, wilt thou serue me, and Ile make thee go like *Qui mihi discipulus?*

Clo. How, in verse?

Wag. No sirra, in beaten silke and stanes acre.

Clo. how, how, knaues acre? I, I thought that was al the land his father left him: Doe yee heare, I would be sorie to robbe you of your liuing.

Wag. Sirra, I say in stanes acre.

Clo. Oho, oho, stanes acre, why then belike, if I were your man, I should be ful of vermine.

Wag. So thou shalt, whether thou beest with me, or no: but sirra, leaue your iesting, and binde your selfe presently vnto me for seauen yeeres, or Ile turne al the lice about thee into familiars, and they shal teare thee in peeces.

Clo. Doe you heare sir? you may saue that labour, they are too familiar with me already, swowns they are as bolde with my flesh, as if they had payd for my meate and drinke.

Wag. wel, do you heare sirra? holde, take these gilders.

Clo. Gridyrons, what be they?

B 3   Wagner

The tragicall History of

Wag. Why french crownes.

Clo. Was but for the name of french crownes a man were as good haue as many english counters, and what should I do with these?

Wag. Why now sirra thou art at an houres warning whensoeuer or wheresoeuer the diuell shall fetch thee.

Clo. No, no, here take your gridirons againe.

Wag. Truly Ile none of them.

Clo. Truly but you shall.

Wag. Beare witnesse I gaue them him.

Clo. Beare witnesse I giue them you againe.

Wag. Well, I will cause two diuels presently to fetch thee away Baliol and Belcher.

Clo. Let your Baliol and your Belcher come here, and Ile knocke them, they were neuer so knockt since they were diuels, say I should kill one of them what would folkes say: do ye see yonder tall fellow in the round slop, hee has kild the diuell, so I should be cald kill diuell all the parish ouer.

Enter two diuells, and the clowne runnes vp and downe crying.

Wag. Baliol and Belcher, spirits away. *Exeunt.*

Clow. What, are they gone? a vengeance on them, they haue vilde long nailes, there was a hee diuell and a shee diuell, Ile tell you how you shall know them, all hee diuels has hornes, and all shee diuels has clifts and clouen feete.

Wag. Well sirra follow me.

Clo. But do you heare? if I should serue you, would you teach me to raise vp Banios and Belcheos?

Wag. I will teach thee to turne thy selfe to any thing, to a dogge, or a catte, or a mouse, or a ratte, or any thing.

Clo. How? a Christian fellow to a dogge or a catte, a mouse or a ratte? no, no sir, if you turne me into any thing, let it be in the likenesse of a little pretie frisking flea, that I may be here and there and euery where, O Ile tickle the pretie wenches plackets Ile be amongst them ifaith.

Wag.

Doctor Faustus.

Wag. Wel sirra, come.
Clo. But doe you heare Wagner?
Wag. How Baioll and Belcher.
Clo. O Lord I pray sir, let Banio and Belcher go sleepe.
Wag. Vilaine, call me Maister Wagner, and let thy left eye be diametarily fixt vpon my right heele, with *quasi vestigias nostras insistere.*   *exit*
Clo. God forgius me, he speakes Dutch fustian: well, Ile folow him, Ile serue him, thats flat.   *exit*

Enter Faustus in his Study.

Fau. Now Faustus must thou needes be damnd,
And canst thou not be saued?
what botes it then to thinke of God or heauen?
Away with such vaine fancies and despaire,
Despaire in God, and trust in Belsabub:
Now go not backeward: no Faustus, be resolute,
Why wauerest thou? O something soundeth in mine eares:
Abiure this Magicke, turne to God againe,
I and Faustus wil turne to God againe.
To God? he loues thee not,
The god thou seruest is thine owne appetite,
Wherein is fixt the loue of Belsabub,
To him Ile build an altare and a church,
And offer luke warme blood of new borne babes.

Enter good Angell, and Euill.

Good Angel Sweet Faustus, leaue that execrable art.
Fau. Contrition, prayer, repentance: what of them?
Good Angel O they are meanes to bring thee vnto heauen.
Euill Angel Rather illusions fruites of lunacy,
That makes men foolish that do trust them most.
Good Angel Sweet Faustus thinke of heauen, and heauenly things.
Euill Angel No Faustus, thinke of honor and wealth.
Fau. Of wealth,   *exeunt.*
Why the signory of Emden shalbe mine,
When Mephastophilus shal stand by me,

what

The tragicall History of

What God can hurt thee Faustus? thou art safe,
Cast no more doubts, come Mephastophilus,
And bring glad tidings from great Lucifer:
Ist not midnight? come Mephastophilus,
Veni veni Mephastophile   *enter Meph:*
Now tel, what sayes Lucifer thy Lord?

Me: That I shal waite on Faustus whilst I liue,
So he wil buy my seruice with his soule.

Fau: Already Faustus hath hazarded that for thee.

Me: But Faustus, thou must bequeathe it solemnely,
And write a deede of gift with thine owne blood,
For that security craues great Lucifer:
If thou deny it, I wil backe to hel.

Fau: Stay Mephastophilus, and tel me, what good wil
my soule do thy Lord?

Me: Inlarge his kingdome.

Fau: Is that the reason he tempts vs thus?

Me: *Solamen miseris socios habuisse doloris.*

Fau: Haue you any paine that tortures others?

Me: As great as haue the humane soules of men:
But tel me Faustus, shal I haue thy soule,
And I wil be thy slaue, and waite on thee,
And giue thee more than thou hast wit to aske.

Fau: I Mephastophilus, I giue it thee.

Me: Then stabbe thine arme couragiously,
And binde thy soule, that at some certaine day
Great Lucifer may claime it as his owne,
And then be thou as great as Lucifer.

Fau: Loe Mephastophilus, for loue of thee,
I cut mine arme, and with my proper blod
Assure my soule to be great Lucifers,
Chiefe Lord and regent of pe. petual night,
View heere the blood that trickles from mine arme,
And let it be propitious for my wish.

Meph: But Faustus, thou must write it in manner of a deede of gift.

Fau. I so I will, but Mephastophilis my bloud conceales

and

Doctor Faustus.

and I can write no more.

    Me. Ile fetch thee fier to diſſolue it ſtraight.   *Exit.*

    Fau. What might the ſtaying of my bloud portend?
Is it vnwilling I ſhould write this bill?
Why ſtreames it not, that I may write afreſh?
Fauſtus giues to thee his ſoule: ah there it ſtayde,
Why ſhouldſt thou not? is not thy ſoule thine owne?
Then write againe, *Fauſtus giues to thee his ſoule.*

    Enter Mephaſtophilis with a chafer of coles.

    Me. Heres fier, come *Fauſtus*, ſet it on.

    Fau. So now the bloud begins to cleare againe,
Now will I make an ende immediately.

    Me. O what will not I do to obtaine his ſoule?

    Fau. Conſummatum eſt, this Bill is ended,
And *Fauſtus* hath bequeath'd his ſoule to *Lucifer*.
But what is this inſcription on mine arme?
Homo fuge, whither ſhould I flie?
If vnto God hee'le throwe thee downe to hell,
My ſences are deceiu'd, here's nothing writ,
I ſee it plaine, here in this place is writ,
Homo fuge, yet ſhall not *Fauſtus* flye.

    Me. Ile fetch him ſomewhat to delight his minde.

                                             exit.

    Enter with diuels, giuing crownes and rich apparell to
        Fauſtus, and daunce, and then depart.

    Fau. Speake *Mephaſtophilis*, what meanes this ſhewe?

    Me. Nothing *Fauſtus*, but to delight thy minde withall,
And to ſhewe thee what Magicke can performe.

    Fau. But may I raiſe vp ſpirits when I pleaſe?

    Me. I *Fauſtus*, and do greater things then theſe.

    Fau. Then theres inough for a thouſand ſoules,
Here *Mephaſtophilis* receiue this ſcrowle,
A deede of gift of body and of ſoule:
But yet conditionally, that thou performe
All articles preſcrib'd betweene vs both.

                                  C   *Me:*

The tragicall History of

Me. Fauſtus, I ſweare by hel and Lucifer
To effect all promiſes betweene vs made.

Fau. Then heare me reade them: on theſe conditions following.

First, that Fauſtus may be a ſpirit in ſorme and ſubſtance.

Secondly, that *Mephaſtophilis* ſhall be his ſeruant, and at
his commaund.

Thirdly, that *Mephaſtophilis* ſhall do for him, and bring
him whatſoeuer.

Fourthly, that hee ſhall be in his chamber or houſe in-
uiſible.

Laſtly, that hee ſhall appeare to the ſaid *Iohn Fauſtus* at all
times, in what forme or ſhape ſoeuer he pleaſe.

I *Iohn Fauſtus* of *Wertenberge*, Doctor, by theſe preſents, do
giue both body and ſoule to *Lucifer* prince of the Eaſt, and his
miniſter *Mephaſtophilis*, and furthermore graunt vnto them,
that 24. yeares being expired, the articles aboue written in-
uiolate, full power to fetch or carry the ſaid *Iohn Fauſtus* body
and ſoule, fleſh, bloud, or goods, into their habitation where-
ſoeuer.

By me Iohn Fauſtus.

Me. Speake Fauſtus, do you deliuer this as your deede?

Fau. I, take it, and the diuell giue thee good on't.

Me. Now Fauſtus aſke what thou wilt.

Fau. First will I queſtion with thee about hell,
Tel me, where is the place that men call hell?

Me. Under the heauens.

Fau. I, but where about?

Me. Within the bowels of theſe elements,
Where we are tortur'd and remaine for euer,
Hell hath no limits, nor is circumſcrib'd
In one ſelfe place, for where we are is hell,
And where hell is, muſt we euer be:
And to conclude, when all the world diſſolues,
And euery creature ſhalbe purifieo,
All places ſhall be hell that is not heauen.

Fau.

Doctor Faustus.

Fau. Come, I thinke hell's a fable.
Me. I, thinke so still, till experience change thy minde.
Fau. Why? thinkst thou then that Faustus shall bee damn'd?
Me. I of necessitie, for here's the scrowle, Wherein thou hast giuen thy soule to Lucifer.
Fau. I, and body too, but what of that?
Thinkst thou that Faustus is so fond,
To imagine, that after this life there is any paine?
Tush these are trifles and meere olde wiues tales.
Me. But Faustus I am an instance to proue the contrary
For I am damnd, and am now in hell.
Fau. How? now in hell? nay and this be hell, Ile willingly be damnd here: what walking, disputing, &c. But leauing off this, let me haue a wife, the fairest maid in Germany, for I am wanton and lasciuious, and can not liue without a wife.
Me. How, a wife? I prithee Faustus talke not of a wife.
Fau. Nay sweete *Mephastophilis* fetch me one, for I will haue one.
Me. Well thou wilt haue one, sit there till I come, Ile fetch thee a wife in the diuels name.

Enter with a diuell drest like a woman,
with fier workes.

Me: Tel Faustus, how dost thou like thy wife?
Fau: A plague on her for a hote whore.
Me: Tut Faustus, marriage is but a ceremoniall toy, if thou louest me, thinke more of it.
Ile cull thee out the fairest curtezans,
And bring them eu'ry morning to thy bed,
She whome thine eie shall like, thy heart shal haue,
Be she as chaste as was Penelope,
As wise as Saba, or as beautiful
As was bright Lucifer before his fall.
Hold, take this booke, peruse it thorowly,
The iterating of these lines brings golde,

C 2   The

The tragicall History of

The framing of this circle on the ground,
Brings whirlewindes, tempests, thunder and lightning.
Pronounce this thrice deuoutly to thy selfe,
And men in armour shal appeare to thee,
Ready to execute what thou desirst.

  Fau: Thankes Mephastophilus, yet faine would I haue a booke wherein I might beholde al spels and incantations, that I might raise vp spirits when I please.

  Me: Here they are in this booke.   *There turne to them*

  Fau: Now would I haue a booke where I might see al characters and planets of the heauens, that I might knowe their motions and dispositions.

  Me: Heere they are too.   *Turne to them*

  Fau: Nay let me haue one booke more, and then I haue done, wherein I might see al plants, hearbes and trees that grow vpon the earth.

  Me, Here they be.

  Fau: O thou art deceiued.

  Me: Tut I warrant thee.   *Turne to them*

  Fau: When I behold the heauens, then I repent,
And curse thee wicked Mephastophilus,
Because thou hast depriu'd me of those ioyes.

  Me: why Faustus,
Thinkst thou heauen is such a glorious thing?
I tel thee tis not halfe so faire as thou,
Or any man that breathes on earth.

  Fau: How prouest thou that?

  Me: It was made for man, therefore is man more excellent.

  Fau: If it were made for man, twas made for me:
I wil renounce this magicke, and repent.

        Enter good Angel, and euill Angel.

  Good An: Faustus, repent yet, God wil pitty thee.

  euill An: Thou art a spirite, God cannot pitty thee.

  Fau: who buzzeth in mine eares I am a spirite?
Be I a diuel, yet God may pitty me,
I God wil pitty me, if I repent.

euill

Doctor Faustus.

euill An: I but Faustus neuer shal repent. *exeunt*
    Fau: My hearts so hardned I cannot repent,
Scarse can I name saluation, faith, or heauen,
But fearful ecchoes thunders in mine eares,
Faustus, thou art damn'd, then swordes and kniues,
Poyson, gunnes, halters, and inuenomd stæle
Are layde before me to dispatch my selfe,
And long ere this I should haue slaine my selfe,
Had not sweete pleasure conquerd deepe dispaire.
Haue not I made blinde Homer sing to me,
Of Alexanders loue, and Enons death,
And hath not he that built the walles of Thebes,
With rauishing sound of his melodious harp
Made musicke with my Mephastophilis,
Why should I dye then, or basely dispaire?
I am resolu'd Faustus shal nere repent,
Come Mephastophilis, let vs dispute againe,
And argue of diuine Astrologie,
Tel me, are there many heauens aboue the Moone?
Are all celestiall bodies but one globe,
As is the substance of this centricke earth?
    Me: As are the elements, such are the spheares,
Mutually folded in each others orbe,
And Faustus all iointly moue vpon one axletrée,
Whose terminine is tearmd the worlds wide pole,
Nor are the names of Saturne, Mars, or Iupiter
Faind, but are erring starres.
    Fau. But tell me, haue they all one motion? both *sin & tempore.*
    Me. All ioyntly moue from East to West in 24. houres
vpon the poles of the world, but differ in their motion vpon
the poles of the Zodiake.
    Fau. Tush, these slender trifles Wagner can decide,
Hath Mephastophilus no greater skill?
Who knowes not the double motion of the plannets?
The first is finisht in a naturall day,
The second thus, as Saturne in 30. yeares, Iupiter in 12.

The tragicall History of

Mars in 4. the Sunne, Venus, and Mercury in a yeare: the Moone in 28. dayes. Tush these are fresh mens suppositions, but tell me, hath euery spheare a dominion or *Intelligentia*?

Me. I.

Fau. How many heauens or spheares are there?

Me. Nine, the seuen planets, the firmament, and the imperiall heauen.

Fau. Well, resolue me in this question, why haue wée not coniunctions, oppositions, aspects, eclipsis, all at one time, but in some yeares we haue more, in some lesse?

Me. *Per inæqualem motum respectu totius.*

Fau. Well, I am answered, tell me who made the world?

Me. I will not.

Fau. Sweete Mephastophilus tell me.

Me. Moue me not, for I will not tell thee.

Fau. Villaine, haue I not bound thée to tel me any thinge

Me. I, that is not against our kingdome, but this is, Thinke thou on hell Faustus, for thou art damn'd.

Fau. Thinke Faustus vpon God that made the world.

Me. Remember this.   *Exit.*

Fau. I, goe accursed spirit to vgly hell, Tis thou hast damn'd distressed Faustus soule: Ist not too late?

Enter good Angell and euill.

euill A. Too late.

good A. Neuer too late, if Faustus can repent.

euill A. If thou repent diuels shall teare thée in péeces.

good A. Repent, & they shal neuer race thy skin. *Exeunt.*

Fau. Ah Christ my Sauiour, séeke to saue distressed Faustus soule.

Enter Lucifer, Belsabub, and Mephastophilus.

Lu. Christ cannot saue thy soule, for he is iust, Theres none but I haue intrest in the same.

Fau: O who art thou that lookst so terrible?

Lu: I am Lucifer, and this is my companion Prince in hel.

Fau: O Faustus, they are come to fetch away thy soule.

Lu:

Lu: We come to tell thee thou dost iniure vs,
Thou talkst of Christ, contrary to thy promise,
Thou shouldst not thinke of God, thinke of the deuill,
And of his dame too.

Fau: Nor will I henceforth: pardon me in this,
And Faustus vowes neuer to looke to heauen,
Neuer to name God, or to pray to him,
To burne his Scriptures, slay his Ministers,
And make my spirites pull his churches downe.

Lu: Do so, and we will highly gratifie thee:
Faustus, we are come from hel to shew thee some pastime:
sit downe, and thou shalt see al the seauen deadly sinnes appeare in their proper shapes.

Fau: That sight will be as pleasing vnto me, as paradise
was to Adam, the first day of his creation.

Lu: Talke not of paradise, nor creation, but marke this
shew, talke of the diuel, and nothing else: come away.

Enter the seauen deadly sinnes.

Now Faustus, examine them of their seueral names and
dispositions.

Fau: What art thou? the first.

Pride I am Pride, I disdaine to haue any parents, I am
like to Ouids flea, I can creepe into euery corner of a wench,
sometimes like a periwig, I sit vpon her brow, or like a fan
of feathers, I kisse her lippes, indeede I doe, what doe I not?
but fie, what a scent is here? Ile not speake an other worde,
except the ground were perfumde and couered with cloth of
arras.

Fau: What art thou? the second.

Coue: I am Couetousnes, begotten of an olde churle, in
an olde leatherne bag: and might I haue my wish, I would
desire, that this house, and all the people in it were turnd to
golde, that I might locke you vppe in my good chest, O my
sweete golde

Fau: What art thou? the third.

Wrath I am Wrath, I had neither father nor mother, I
leapt out of a lions mouth, when I was scarce halfe an houre
olde,

The tragicall History of

olde, and euer since I haue runne vp and downe the worlde, with this case of rapiers wounding my selfe, when I had no body to fight withal: I was borne in hel, and looke to it, for some of you shalbe my father.

Fau: what art thou? the fourth.

Enuy I am Envy, begotten of a Chimney-sweeper, and an Oyster wife, I cannot reade, and therefore wish al bookes were burnt: I am leane with seeing others eate, O that there would come a famine through all the worlde, that all might die, and I liue alone, then thou shouldst see how fatt I would be: but must thou sit and I stand? come downe with a vengeance.

Fau: Away enuious rascall: what art thou? the fift.

Glut: who I sir, I am Gluttony, my parents are al dead, and the diuel a peny they haue left me, but a bare pention, and that is 30. meales a day, and tenne beauers, a small trifle to suffice nature, O I come of a royall parentage, my grandfather was a gammon of bacon, my grandmother a hogs head of Claret-wine: My godfathers were these, Peter Pickle-herring, and Martin Martlemas-biefe, O but my godmother she was a iolly gentlewoman, and welbeloued in euery good towne and Citie, her name was mistresse Margery March-beere: now Faustus, thou hast heard all my Progeny, wilt thou bid me to supper?

Fau. No, Ile see thee hanged, thou wilt eate vp all my victualls.

Glut. Then the diuell choake thee.

Fau. Choake thy selfe glutton: what art thou? the sixt.

Sloath. I am sloath, I was begotten on a sunny banke, where I haue laine euer since, and you haue done me great iniury to bring me from thence, let me be carried thither againe by Gluttony and Leachery, Ile not speake an other word for a kings ransome.

Fau. What are you mistresse minkes? the seauenth and last.

Lechery Who I sir? I am one that loues an inch of raw Mutton better then an ell of fride stock-fish, and the first

letter

Doctor Faustus.

letter of my name beginnes with leachery.

  Away, to hel, to hel.   *exeunt the sinnes.*

 Lu. Now Faustus, how dost thou like this?

 Fau: O this feedes my soule.

 Lu. But Faustus, in hel is al manner of delight.

 Fau. O might I see hel, and returne againe, how happy were I then?

 Lu. Thou shalt, I wil send for thee at midnight, in mean time take this booke, peruse it throwly, and thou shalt turne thy selfe into what shape thou wilt.

 Fau. Great thankes mighty Lucifer, this wil I keepe as chary as my life.

 Lu. Farewel Faustus, and thinke on the diuel.

 Fau. Farewel great Lucifer, come Mephastophilis.

    exeunt omnes.

    enter Wagner solus.

Wag. Learned Faustus,
To know the secrets of Astronomy,
Grauen in the booke of Ioues his firmament,
Did mount himselfe to scale Olympus top,
Being seated in a chariot burning bright,
Drawne by the strength of yoky dragons neckes,
He now is gone to proue Cosmography,
And as I guesse, wil first ariue at Rome,
To see the Pope, and manner of his court,
And take some part of holy Peters feast,
That to this day is highly solemnizd. *exit Wagner*

   Enter Faustus and Mephastophilus.

 Fau. Hauing now, my good Mephastophilus,
Past with delight the stately towne of Trier,
Inuirond round with ayrie mountaine tops,
With walles of flint, and deepe intrenched lakes,
Not to be wonne by any conquering prince,
From Paris next coasting the Realme of France,
Wee sawe the riuer Maine fall into Rhine,
Whose bankes are set with groues of fruitful vines.
Then vp to Naples, rich Campania,

    D   whose

The tragicall History of

Whose buildings faire and gorgeous to the eye,
The streetes straight forth, and pau'd with finest bricke,
Quarters the towne in foure equiuolence.
There sawe we learned Maroes golden tombe,
The way he cut an English mile in length,
Thorough a rocke of stone in one nights space.
From thence to Venice, Padua, and the rest,
In midst of which a sumptuous Temple stands,
That threats the starres with her aspiring toppe.
Thus hitherto hath Faustus spent his time,
But tell me now, what resting place is this?
Hast thou as erst I did commaund,
Conducted me within the walles of Rome?

   Me. Faustus I haue, and because we wil not be vnprouided, I haue taken vp his holinesse priuy chamber for our vse.

   Fau. I hope his holinesse will bid vs welcome. (cheare,
   Me. Tut, tis no matter man, weele be bold with his good
And now my Faustus, that thou maist perceiue
What Rome containeth to delight thee with,
Know that this Citie stands vpon seuen hilles
That vnderprops the groundworke of the same,
Ouer the which foure stately bridges leane,
That makes safe passage to each part of Rome.
Upon the bridge call'd Ponto Angelo,
Erected is a Castle passing strong,
Within whose walles such store of ordonance are,
And double Canons, fram'd of carued brasse,
As match the dayes within one compleate yeare,
Besides the gates and high piramides,
Which Iulius Cæsar brought from Affrica.

   Fau. Now by the kingdomes of infernall rule,
Of Styx, Acheron, and the fiery lake
Of euer-burning Phlegiton I sweare,
That I do long to see the monuments
And scituation of bright splendant Rome,
Come therefore lets away.

                                           Me:

Doctor Faustus.

Me. Nay Faustus stay, I know youd faine see the Pope,
And take some part of holy Peters feast,
Where thou shalt see a troupe of bald-pate Friers,
Whose *summum bonum* is in belly-cheare.

Fau. Well, I am content, to compasse then some sport,
And by their folly make vs merriment,
Then charme me that I may be inuisble, to do what I
please vnsœne of any whilst I stay in Rome.

Me. So Faustus, now do what thou wilt, thou shalt not
be discerned.

*Sound a Sonnet, enter the Pope and the Cardinall of Lorraine
to the banket, with Friers attending.*

Pope. My Lord of Lorraine, wilt please you draw neare.

Fau. Fall too, and the diuel choake you and you spare.

Pope. How now, whose that which spake? Friers looke
about.

Fri. Heere's no body, if it like your Holynesse.

Pope. My Lord, here is a daintie dish was sent me from
the Bishop of Millaine.

Fau. I thanke you sir.   *Snatch it.*

Pope. How now, whose that which snatcht the meate
from me? will no man looke?
My Lord, this dish was sent me from the Cardinall of Florence.

Fau. You say true, Ile hafe.

Pope. What againe? my Lord Ile drinke to your grace

Fau. Ile pledge your grace.

Lor. My Lord, it may be some ghost newly crept out of
Purgatory come to begge a pardon of your holinesse.

Pope It may be so, Friers prepare a dirge to lay the fury
of this ghost, once againe my Lord fall too.

The Pope crosseth himselfe.

Fau. What, are you crossing of your selfe?
Well vse that tricke no more, I would aduise you.

Crosse againe.

Fau. Well, theres the second time, aware the third,
I giue you faire warning.

D 2   *Crosse*

The tragicall History of

Crosse againe, and Faustus hits him a boxe of the eare, and they all runne away.

Fau: Come on Mephastophilis, what shall we do?

Me. Nay I know not, we shalbe curst with bell, booke, and candle.

Fau. How? bell, booke, and candle, candle, booke, and bell, Forward and backward, to curse Faustus to hell. Anon you shal heare a hogge grunt, a calfe bleate, and an asse braye, because it is S. Peters holy day.

Enter all the Friers to sing the Dirge.

Frier. Come brethren, lets about our businesse with good deuotion.

Sing this. Cursed be hee that stole away his holinesse meare from the table. *maledicat dominus.*

Cursed be hee that strooke his holinesse a blowe on the face.
maledicat dominus.

Cursed be he that tooke Frier Sandelo a blow on the pate.
male, &c.

Cursed be he that disturbeth our holy Dirge.
male, &c.

Cursed be he that tooke away his holinesse wine.
maledicat dominus.

Et omnes sancti Amen.

Beate the Friers, and fling fier-workes among them, and so Exeunt.

Enter Chorus.

When Faustus had with pleasure tane the view
Of rarest things, and royal courts of kings,
Hee stayde his course, and so returned home,
Where such as beare his absence, but with griefe,
I meane his friends and nearest companions,
Did gratulate his safetie with kinde words,
And in their conference of what befell,
Touching his iourney through the world and ayre,
They put forth questions of Astrologie,

which

Doctor Faustus.

Which Faustus answerd with such learned skill,
As they admirde and wondred at his wit.
Now is his fame spread forth in euery land,
Amongst the rest the Emperour is one,
Carolus the fift, at whose pallace now
Faustus is feasted mongst his noblemen.
What there he did in triall of his art,
I leaue vntold, your eyes shall see performd. *Exit.*

Enter Robin the Ostler with a booke in his hand

Robin O this is admirable! here I ha stolne one of doctor Faustus coniuring books, and ifaith I meane to search some circles for my owne vse: now wil I make al the maidens in our parish dance at my pleasure starke naked before me, and so by that meanes I shal see more then ere I felt, or saw yet.

Enter Rafe calling Robin.

Rafe Robin, prethee come away, theres a Gentleman tarries to haue his horse, and he would haue his things rubd and made cleane: he keepes such a chafing with my mistris about it, and she has sent me to looke thee out, prethee come away.

Robin Keepe out, keep out, or else you are blowne vp, you are dismembred Rafe, keepe out, for I am about a roaring peece of worke.

Rafe Come, what doest thou with that same booke thou canst not reade?

Robin Yes, my maister and mistris shal finde that I can reade, he for his forehead, she for her priuate study, shee's borne to beare with me, or else my Art failes.

Rafe Why Robin what booke is that?

Robin What booke? why the most intollerable booke for coniuring that ere was inuented by any brimstone diuel.

Rafe Canst thou coniure with it?

Robin I can do al these things easily with it: first, I can make thee druncke with ipocrase at any taberne in Europe for nothing, thats one of my coniuring workes.

Rafe Our maister Parson sayes thats nothing.

Robin True Rafe, and more Rafe, if thou hast any mind

The tragicall History of

to Nan Spit our kitchin maide, then turne her and wind her to thy owne vse, as often as thou wilt, and at midnight.

Rafe O braue Robin, shal I haue Nan Spit, and to mine owne vse? On that condition Ile feede thy diuel with horse-bread as long as he liues, of free cost.

Robin No more sweete Rafe, letts goe and make cleane our bootes which lie foule vpon our handes, and then to our coniuring in the diuels name. *exeunt.*

Enter Robin and Rafe with a siluer Goblet.

Robin Come Rafe, did not I tell thee, we were for euer made by this doctor Faustus booke? *ecce signum,* heeres a simple purchase for horse-keepers, our horses shal eate no hay as long as this lasts. *enter the Vintner.*

Rafe But Robin, here comes the vintner.

Robin Hush, Ile gul him supernaturally: Drawer, I hope al is payd, God be with you, come Rafe.

Vintn. Soft sir, a word with you, I must yet haue a goblet payde from you ere you goe.

Robin I a goblet Rafe, I a goblet? I scorne you: and you are but a &c. I a goblet? search me.

Vintn. I meane so sir with your fauor.

Robin How say you now?

Vintner I must say somewhat to your felow, you sir.

Rafe Me sir, me sir, search your fill: now sir, you may be ashamed to burden honest men with a matter of truth.

Vintner Wel, tone of you hath this goblet about you.

Ro. You lie Drawer, tis afore me: sirra you, Ile teach ye to impeach honest men: stand by, Ile scowre you for a goblet, stand aside you had best, I charge you in the name of Belzabub: looke to the goblet Rafe.

Vintner what meane you sirra?

Robin Ile tel you what I meane. *He reades.*
Sanctobulorum Periphrasticon: nay Ile tickle you Vintner, looke to the goblet Rafe, *Polypragmos Belseborams framanto pacostiphos tostu Mephastophilis, &c.*

Enter Mephostophilis: sets squibs at their backes:
they runne about.

Vintner

Doctor Faustus.

Vintner O *nomine Domine*, what meanst thou Robin, thou hast no goblet.

Rafe Peccatum peccatorum, heeres thy goblet, good Vintner.

Robin Misericordia pro nobis, what shal I doe? good diuel forgiue me now, and Ile neuer rob thy Libzary moze.

Enter to them Meph.

Meph. Vanish vilaines, th'one like an Ape, an other like a Beare, the third an Asse, for doing this enterprise.
Monarch of hel, vnder whose blacke suruey
Great Potentates do kneele with awful feare,
Upon whose altars thousand soules do lie,
How am I vexed with these vilaines charmes?
From Constantinople am I hither come,
Onely for pleasure of these damned slaues.

Robin How, from Constantinople? you haue had a great iourney, wil you take sixe pence in your purse to pay for your supper, and be gone?

Me. wel villaines, for your presumption, I transforme thee into an Ape, and thee into a Dog, and so be gone. *exit.*

Rob. How, into an Ape? thats braue, Ile haue fine sport with the boyes, Ile get nuts and apples enow.

Rafe And I must be a Dogge. *exeunt.*

Robin Ifaith thy head wil neuer be out of the potage pot.

Enter Emperour, Faustus, and a Knight,
with Attendants.

Em. Maister doctor Faustus, I haue heard strange report of thy knowledge in the blacke Arte, how that none in my Empire, nor in the whole world can compare with thee, for the rare effects of Magicke: they say thou hast a familiar spirit, by whome thou canst accomplish what thou list, this therefore is my request, that thou let me see some proofe of thy skil, that mine eies may be witnesses to confirme what mine eares haue heard reported, and here I sweare to thee, by the honor of mine Imperial crowne, that what euer thou doest, thou shalt be no wayes preiudiced or indamaged.

Knight Ifaith he lookes much like a coniurer. *afide.*

Fau.

31

The tragicall History of

Fau. My gratious Soueraigne, though I must confesse my selfe farre inferior to the report men haue published, and nothing answerable to the honor of your Imperial maiesty, yet for that loue and duety bindes me thereunto, I am content to do whatsoeuer your maiesty shall command me.

Em. Then doctor Faustus, marke what I shall say, As I was sometime solitary set, within my Closet, sundry thoughts arose, about the honour of mine aunceftors, howe they had wonne by prowesse such exploits, gote such riches, subdued so many kingdomes, as we that do succœde, or they that shal hereafter possesse our throne, shal (I feare me) neuer attaine to that degrée of high renowne and great authoritie, amongest which kings is Alexander the great, chiefe spectacle of the worldes preheminence,

The bright shining of whose glorious actes
Lightens the world with his reflecting beames,
As when I heare but motion made of him,
It grieues my soule I neuer saw the man:
If therefore thou, by cunning of thine Art,
Canst raise this man from hollow vaults below,
Where lies intombde this famous Conquerour,
And bring with him his beauteous Paramour,
Both in their right shapes, gesture, and attire
They vsde to weare during their time of life,
Thou shalt both satisfie my iust desire,
And giue me cause to praise thée whilst I liue.

Fau: My gratious Lord, I am ready to accomplish your request, so farre forth as by art and power of my spirit I am able to performe.

Knight Faith thats iust nothing at all.   *aside.*

Fau. But if it like your Grace, it is not in my abilitie to present before your eyes, the true substantiall bodies of those two deceased princes which long since are consumed to dust.

Knight I mary master doctor, now thores a signe of grace in you, when you wil confesse the trueth.   *aside.*

Fau: But such spirites as can liuely resemble Alexander and his Paramour, shal appeare before your Grace, in that
                                                                manner

Doctor Faustus.

manner that they best liu'd in, in their most florishing estate, which I doubt not shal sufficiently content your Imperiall maiesty.

Em. Go to maister Doctor, let me see them presently.

Kn. Do you heare maister Doctor, you bring Alexander and his paramour before the emperor?

Fau. How then sir?

Kn. Ifaith thats as true as Diana turnd me to a stag.

Fau: No sir, but when Acteon died, he left the hornes for you: Mephastophilis be gone. *exit Meph.*

Kn. Nay, and you go to coniuring, Ile be gone. *exit Kn:*

Fau. Ile meete with you anone for interrupting me so: heere they are my gratious Lord.

Enter Meph: with Alexander and his paramour.

emp. Maister Doctor, I heard this Lady while she liu'd had a wart or moale in her necke, how shal I know whether it be so or no?

Fau: Your highnes may boldly go and see. *exit Alex:*

emp: Sure these are no spirites, but the true substantiall bodies of those two deceased princes.

Fau: Wilt please your highnes now to send for the knight that was so pleasant with me here of late?

emp: One of you call him foorth.

Enter the Knight with a paire of hornes on his head.

emp. How now sir knight? why I had thought thou hadst boene a batcheler, but now I see thou hast a wife, that not only giues thee hornes, but makes thee weare them, feele on thy head.

Kn: Thou damned wretch, and execrable dogge,
Bred in the concaue of some monstrous rocke:
How darst thou thus abuse a Gentleman?
Villaine I say, vndo what thou hast done.

E   Faustus

The tragicall History of

Fau: O not so fast sir, theres no haste but good, are you remembred how you crossed me in my conference with the emperour? I thinke I haue met with you for it.

emp: Good Maister Doctor, at my intreaty release him, he hath done penance sufficient.

Fau: My Gratious Lord, not so much for the iniury hée offred me héere in your presence, as to delight you with some mirth, hath *Faustus* worthily requited this iniurious knight, which being all I desire, I am content to release him of his hornes: and sir knight, hereafter speake well of Scholers: Mephastophilis, transforme him strait. Now my good Lord hauing done my duety, I humbly take my leaue.

emp: Farewel maister Doctor, yet ere you goe, expect from me a bounteous reward.   *exit Emperour.*

Fau: Now Mephastophilis, the restlesse course that time doth runne with calme and silent foote,
Shortning my dayes and thred of vitall life,
Calls for the payment of my latest yeares,
Therefore sweet Mephastophilis, let vs make haste to Wertenberge.

Me: what, wil you goe on horse backe, or on foote?

Fau: Nay, til I am past this faire and pleasant gréene, ile walke on foote.   *enter a Horse-courser*

Hors: I haue béene al this day séeking one maister Fustian: masse sée where he is, God saue you maister doctor.

Fau: What horse-courser, you are wel met.

Hors: Do you heare sir? I haue brought you forty dollers for your horse.

Fau: I cannot sel him so: if thou likst him for fifty, take him.

Hors: Alas sir, I haue no more, I pray you speake for me.

Me: I pray you let him haue him, he is an honest felow, and he has a great charge, neither wife nor childe.

Fau: Wel, come giue me your money, my boy wil deliuer him to you: but I must tel you one thing before you haue him,

Doctor Faustus.

him, ride him not into the water at any hand.

Hors: why sir, wil he not drinke of all waters?

Fau: O yes, he wil drinke of al waters, but ride him not into the water, ride him ouer hedge or ditch, or where thou wilt, but not into the water.

Hors: Wel sir, Now am I made man for euer, Ile not leaue my horse for fortie: if he had but the qualitie of hey ding, ding, hey, ding, ding, Ide make a braue liuing on him; hee has a buttocke as slicke as an Ele: wel god buy sir, your boy wil deliuer him me: but hark ye sir, if my horse be sick, or ill at ease, if I bring his water to you, youle tel me what it is?
Exit Horsecourser.

Fau. Away you villaine: what, dost thinke I am a horse-doctor? what art thou Faustus but a man condemnd to die? Thy fatall time doth drawe to finall ende,
Dispaire doth driue distrust vnto my thoughts,
Confound these passions with a quiet sleepe:
Tush, Christ did call the thiefe vpon the Crosse,
Then rest thee Faustus quiet in conceit. *Sleepe in his chaire.*

Enter Horsecourser all wet, crying.

Horf. Alas, alas, Doctor Fustian quoth a, mas Doctor Lopus was neuer such a Doctor, has giuen me a purgation, has purg'd me of fortie Dollers, I shall neuer see them more: but yet like an asse as I was, I would not be ruled by him, for he bade me I should ride him into no water: now, I thinking my horse had had some rare qualitie that he would not haue had me knowne of, I like a ventrous youth, rid him into the deepe pond at the townes ende, I was no sooner in the middle of the pond, but my horse vanisht away, and I sat vpon a bottle of hey, neuer so neare drowning in my life: but Ile seeke out my Doctor, and haue my fortie dollers againe, or Ile make it the dearest horse: O yonder is his snipper snapper, do you heare? you, hey, passe, where's your maister?

E 2 Me.

The tragicall History of

Me. Why sir, what would you: you cannot speake with him.

Hors. But I wil speake with him.

Me. Why hée's fast asléepe, come some other time.

Hors. Ile speake with him now, or Ile breake his glasse-windowes about his eares.

Me. I tell thée he has not slept this eight nights.

Hors. And he haue not slept this eight wéekes Ile speake with him.

Me. Sée where he is fast asléepe.

Hors. I, this is he, God saue ye maister doctor, maister doctor, maister doctor Fustian, fortie dollers, fortie dollers for a bottle of hey.

Me. Why, thou séest he heares thée not.

Hors. So, ho, ho : so, ho, ho.   *Hallow in his eare.*

No, will you not wake? Ile make you wake ere I goe.

Pull him by the legge, and pull it away.

Alas, I am vndone, what shall I do :

Fau. O my legge, my legge, helpe Mephastophilis, call the Officers, my legge, my legge.

Me. Come villaine to the Constable.

Hors. O Lord sir, let me goe, and Ile giue you fortie dollers more.

Me. Where be they?

Hors. I haue none about me, come to my Ostrie and Ile giue them you.

Me. Be gone quickly.   *Horsecourser runnes away.*

Fau. What is he gone? farwel he, Faustus has his legge againe, and the Horsecourler I take it, a bottle of hey for his labour; wel, this tricke shal cost him fortie dollers more.

Enter Wagner.

How now Wagner, what's the newes with thée?

Wag.

Doctor Faustus.

Wag. Sir, the Duke of Vanholt doth earnestly entreate your company.

Fau. The Duke of Vanholt! an honourable gentleman, to whom I must be no niggard of my cunning, come Mephastophilis, let's away to him. *exeunt.*

Enter to them the Duke, and the Dutches, the Duke speakes.

Du: Beléeue me maister Doctor, this merriment hath much pleased me.

Fau: My gratious Lord, I am glad it contents you so wel : but it may be Madame, you take no delight in this, I haue heard that great bellied women do long for some dainties or other, what is it Madame? tell me, and you shal haue it.

Dutch. Thankes, good maister doctor,
And for I sée your curteous intent to pleasure me, I wil not hide from you the thing my heart desires, and were it nowe summer, as it is January, and the dead time of the winter, I would desire no better meate then a dish of ripe grapes.

Fau: Alas Madame, thats nothing, Mephastophilis, be gone: *exit Meph.* were it a greater thing then this, so it would content you, you should haue it *enter Mephasto:* here they be madam, wilt please you taste *with the grapes.* on them.

Du: Beléeue me maister Doctor, this makes me wonder aboue the rest, that being in the dead time of winter, and in the month of January, how you shuld come by these grapes.

Fau: If it like your grace, the yéere is diuided into two circles ouer the whole worlde, that when it is héere winter with vs, in the contrary circle it is summer with them, as in India, Saba, and farther countries in the East, and by means of a swift spirit that I haue, I had them brought hither, as ye sé, how do you like them Madame, be they good?

Du: Beléeue me Maister doctor, they be the best grapes

E 3 that

The tragicall History of

that ere I tasted in my life before.

   Fau: I am glad they content you so Madam.

   Du: Come Madame, let vs in, where you must wel reward this learned man for the great kindnes he hath shewd to you.

   Dut: And so I wil my Lord, and whilst I liue,
Rest beholding for this curtesie.

   Fau: I humbly thanke your Grace.

   Du: Come, maister Doctor follow vs, and receiue your reward.   *exeunt.*

          enter Wagner solus.

   Wag. I thinke my maister meanes to die shortly,
For he hath giuen to me al his goodes,
And yet me thinkes, if that death were neere,
He would not banquet, and carowse, and swill
Amongst the Students, as euen now he doth,
Who are at supper with such belly-cheere,
As Wagner nere beheld in all his life.
See where they come: belike the feast is ended.

      Enter Faustus with two or three Schollers

   1. Sch. Maister Doctor Faustus, since our conference about faire Ladies, which was the beutifulst in all the world, we haue determined with our selues, that Helen of *Greece* was the admirablest Lady that euer liued: therefore master Doctor, if you wil do vs that fauor, as to let vs see that peerelesse Dame of *Greece*, whome al the world admires for maiesty, wee should thinke our selues much beholding vnto you.

   Fau. Gentlemen, for that I know your friendship is vnfained, and Faustus custome is not to denie the iust requests of those that wish him well, you shall behold that pearelesse Dame of Greece, no other waies for pompe and maiestie, then when sir Paris crost the seas with her, and brought the spoiles to rich Dardania. Be silent then, for danger is in words.

                                                    Mu-

Doctor Faustus.

Musicke sounds, and Helen passeth ouer the Stage.

2. Sch. Too simple is my wit to tell her praise,
Whom all the world admires for maiestie.

3. Sch. No maruel tho the angry Greekes pursude
With tenne yeares warre the rape of such a queene,
Whose heauenly beauty passeth all compare.

1. Since we haue seene the pride of natures workes,
And onely Paragon of excellence, *Enter an*
Let vs depart, and for this glorious deed *old man.*
Happy and blest be Faustus euermore.

Fau. Gentlemen farwel, the same I wish to you.
Exeunt Schollers.

Old. Ah Doctor Faustus, that I might preuaile,
To guide thy steps vnto the way of life,
By which sweete path thou maist attaine the gole
That shall conduct thee to celestial rest.
Breake heart, drop bloud, and mingle it with teares,
Teares falling from repentant heauinesse
Of thy most vilde and loathsome filthinesse,
The stench whereof corrupts the inward soule
With such flagitious crimes of hainous sinnes,
As no commiseration may expel,
But mercie Faustus of thy Sauiour sweete,
Whose bloud alone must wash away thy guilt.

Fau. Where art thou Faustus? wretch what hast thou
Damnd art thou Faustus, damnd, dispaire and die, (done?
Hell calls for right, and with a roaring voyce
Sayes, Faustus come, thine houre is come, *Mepha. giues*
And Faustus will come to do thee right. *him a dagger.*

Old. Ah stay good Faustus, stay thy desperate steps,
I see an Angell houers ore thy head,
And with a violl full of precious grace,
Offers to powre the same into thy soule,
Then call for mercie and auoyd dispaire.

Fau. Ah my sweete friend, I feele thy words

The tragicall History of

To comfort my distressed soule,
Leaue me a while to ponder on my sinnes.

   Old. I goe sweete Faustus, but with heauy cheare,
fearing the ruine of thy hopelesse soule.

   Fau. Accursed Faustus, where is mercie now?
I do repent, and yet I do dispaire:
Hell striues with grace for conquest in my breast,
What shal I do to shun the snares of death?

   Me. Thou traitor Faustus, I arrest thy soule
For disobedience to my soueraigne Lord,
Reuolt, or Ile in peece-meale teare thy flesh.

   Fau: Sweete Mephastophilis, intreate thy Lord
To pardon my vniust presumption,
And with my blood againe I wil confirme
My former vow I made to Lucifer.

   Me. Do it then quickely, with vnfained heart,
Lest greater danger do attend thy drift.

   Fau: Torment sweete friend, that base and crooked age,
That durst disswade me from thy Lucifer,
With greatest torments that our hel affords.

   Me: His faith is great, I cannot touch his soule,
But what I may afflict his body with,
I wil attempt, which is but little worth.

   Fau: One thing, good seruant, let me craue of thee
To glut the longing of my hearts desire,
That I might haue vnto my paramour,
That heauenly Helen which I saw of late,
Whose sweete imbracings may extinguish cleane
These thoughts that do disswade me from my vow,
And keepe mine oath I made to Lucifer.

   Me. Faustus, this, or what else thou shalt desire,
Shalbe performde in twinckling of an eie.   *enter Helen.*

   Fau: Was this the face that lancht a thousand shippes?
And burnt the toplesse Towres of Ilium?
Sweete Helen, make me immortall with a kisse:
Her lips suckes forth my soule, see where it flies:
                                                  Come

Doctor Faustus.

Come Helen, come giue mée my soule againe.
Here wil I dwel, for heauen be in these lips,
And all is drosse that is not Helena: *enter old man*
I wil be Paris, and for loue of thée,
Insteede of *Troy* shal *Wertenberge* be sackt,
And I wil combate with weake Menelaus,
And weare thy colours on my plumed Crest:
Yea I wil wound Achillis in the héele,
And then returne to Helen for a kisse.
O thou art fairer then the euening aire,
Clad in the beauty of a thousand starres,
Brighter art thou then flaming Iupiter,
When he appeard to haplesse Semele,
More louely then the monarke of the skie
In wanton Arethusaes azurde armes,
And none but thou shalt be my paramour. *Exeunt.*

Old man Accursed Faustus, miserable man,
That from thy soule excludst the grace of heauen,
And fliest the throne of his tribunall seate,

Enter the Diuelles.

Sathan begins to sift me with his pride,
As in this furnace God shal try my faith,
My faith, vile hel, shal triumph ouer thée,
Ambitious fiends, sée how the heauens smiles
At your repulse, and laughs your state to scorne,
Hence hel, for hence I flie vnto my God. *Exeunt.*

Enter Faustus with the Schollers.

Fau: Ah Gentlemen!
1. Sch: what ailes Faustus?
Fau: Ah my swéete chamber-fellow! had I liued with
thée, then had I liued stil, but now I die eternally: looke,
comes he not? comes he not?
2. Sch: what meanes Faustus?
3. Scholler Belike he is growne into some sickenesse, by
being

F

The tragicall History of

being euer solitary.

   1. Sch: If it be so, weele haue Physitians to cure him, tis but a surffet, neuer feare man.

   Fau: A surffet of deadly sinne that hath damnd both body and soule.

   2. Sch. Yet Faustus looke vp to heauen, remember gods mercies are infinite.

   Fau. But Faustus offence can nere be pardoned, The Serpent that tempted Eue may be sau'd, But not Faustus: Ah Gentlemen, heare me with patience, and tremble not at my speeches, though my heart pants and quiuers to remember that I haue beene a student here these thirty yeeres, O would I had neuer seene Wertenberge, neuer read booke: and what wonders I haue done, al Germany can witnes, yea all the world, for which Faustus hath lost both Germany, and the world, yea heauen it selfe, heauen the seate of God, the throne of the blessed, the kingdome of ioy, and must remaine in hel for euer, hel, ah hel for euer, sweete friends, what shall become of Faustus, being in hel for euer?

   3. Sch. Yet Faustus call on God.

   Fau. On God whome Faustus hath abiur'd, on God, whome Faustus hath blasphemed, ah my God, I would weepe, but the diuel drawes in my teares, gush forth blood, insteade of teares, yea life and soule, Oh he stayes my toug, I would lift vp my hands, but see, they hold them, they hold them.

   All Who Faustus?

   Fau. Lucifer and Mephastophilis. Ah Gentlemen! I gaue them my soule for my cunning.

   All God forbid.

   Fau. God forbade it indeede, but Faustus hath done it: for vaine pleasure of 24. yeares, hath Faustus lost eternall ioy and felicitie, I writ them a bill with mine owne blood, the date is expired, the time wil come, and he wil fetch mee.

   1. Schol. Why did not Faustus tel vs of this before, that Diuines might haue prayed for thee?

   Fau.

Doctor Faustus.

Fau. Oft haue I thought to haue done so, but the diuell threatned to teare mee in peeces, if I namde God, to fetch both body and soule, if I once gaue eare to diuinitie: and now tis too late: Gentlemen away, lest you perish with me.

2. Sch. O what shal we do to Faustus?

Faustus Talke not of me, but saue your selues, and depart.

3. Sch. God wil strengthen me, I wil stay with Faustus.

1. Sch. Tempt not God, sweete friend, but let vs into the next roome, and there pray for him.

Fau. I pray for me, pray for me, and what noyse soeuer yee heare, come not vnto me, for nothing can rescue me.

2. Sch. Pray thou, and we wil pray that God may haue mercy vpon thee.

Fau. Gentlemen farewel, if I liue til morning, Ile visite you: if not, Faustus is gone to hel.

All Faustus, farewel.   *Exeunt Sch.*

The clocke strikes eleauen.

Fau. Ah Faustus,
Now hast thou but one bare hower to liue,
And then thou must be damnd perpetually:
Stand stil you euer mouing spheres of heauen,
That time may cease, and midnight neuer come:
Faire Natures eie, rise, rise againe, and make
Perpetuall day, or let this houre be but a yeare,
A moneth, a weeke, a naturall day,
That Faustus may repent and saue his soule,
O lente lente curité noctis equi:
The starres moue stil, time runs, the clocke wil strike,
The diuel wil come, and Faustus must be damnd.
O Ile leape vp to my God: who pulles me downe?
See see where Christs blood streames in the firmament,
One drop would saue my soule, halfe a drop, ah my Christ,
Ah rend not my heart for naming of my Christ,
Yet wil I call on him, oh spare me Lucifer!

F 2   where

The tragicall History of

Where is it nowe tis gone:
And see where God stretcheth out his arme,
And bends his irefull browes:
Mountaines and hilles, come come, and fall on me,
And hide me from the heauy wrath of God.
No no, then wil I headlong runne into the earth:
Earth gape, O no, it wil not harbour me:
You starres that raignd at my natiuitie,
Whose influence hath alotted death and hel,
Now draw vp Faustus like a foggy mist,
Into the intrailes of yon labring cloude,
That when you vomite forth into the ayre,
My limbes may issue from your smoaky mouthes,
So that my soule may but ascend to heauen:
Ah, halfe the houre is past: *The watch strikes.*
Twil all be past anone:
Oh God, if thou wilt not haue mercy on my soule,
Yet for Chrifts sake, whose bloud hath ransomd me,
Impose some end to my incessant paine,
Let Faustus liue in hel a thousand yeeres.
A hundred thousand, and at last be sau'd.
O no end is limited to damned soules,
Why wert thou not a creature wanting soule?
Or, why is this immortall that thou hast?
Ah Pythagoras *metem su cossis* were that true,
This soule should flie from me, and I be changde
Unto some brutish beast: al beasts are happy, for when they
Their soules are soone dissolud in elements,   (die,
But mine must liue still to be plagde in hel:
Curst be the parents that ingendred me:
No Faustus, curse thy selfe, curse Lucifer,
That hath depriude thee of the ioyes of heauen:
         The clocke striketh twelue.
O it strikes, it strikes, now body turne to ayre,
Or Lucifer wil beare thee quicke to hel:
         Thunder and lightning.

                           Oh

Doctor Faustus.

Oh soule, be changde into little water drops,
And fal into the Ocean, nere be found:
My God, my God, looke not so fierce on me: *Enter diuels.*
Adders, and Serpents, let me breathe a while:
Ugly hell gape not, come not Lucifer,
Ile burne my bookes, ah Mephastophilis.   *exeunt with him*

Enter Chorus.

Cut is the branch that might haue growne ful straight,
And burned is Apolloes Laurel bough,
That sometime grew within this learned man:
Faustus is gone, regard his hellish fall,
Whose fiendful fortune may exhort the wise,
Onely to wonder at vnlawful things,
whose deepenesse doth intise such forward wits,
To practise more than heauenly power permits.

Terminat hora diem, Terminat Author opus.

1520

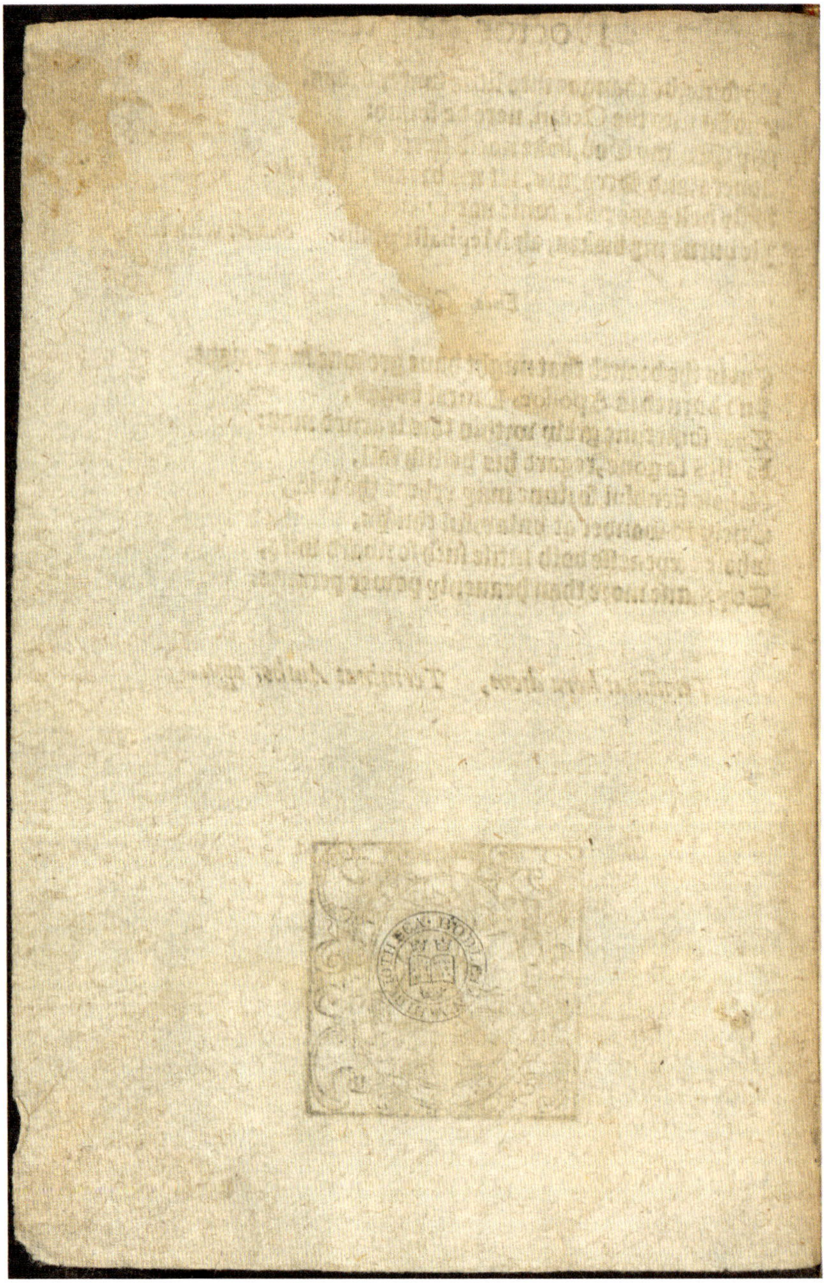